The Superman Syndrome

The Struggles and Pitfalls of Superhero Ministry

Chad Mitchell

With Sheri Bennett

Illustrations by Justin Leifeste

rev/press

Mobile, Alabama

The Superman Syndrome by Chad Mitchell with Sheri Bennett
Copyright © 2009 Chad Mitchell

All rights reserved. This book is protected under the copyright laws of the United States of America. This book may not be copied or reprinted for commercial gain or profit.

Scripture quotations marked NIV are taken from *THE HOLY BIBLE: New International Version* ©1978 by the New York International Bible Society, used by permission of Zondervan Bible Publishers.

Scriptures marked MSG are taken from *THE MESSAGE*. Copyright © by Eugene H. Peterson 1993, 1994, 1995, 1996, 2000, 2002. Used by permission of NavPress Publishing Group.

Scriptures marked NAS are taken from the *New American Standard Bible*, Copyright ©1960, 1962, 1963, 1968, 1971, 1973, 1975, 1977 by The Lockman Foundation. Scripture marked NKJ are taken from the New King James Version. Copyright © 1982 by Thomas Nelson, Inc.

Scripture marked NLT are taken from the Holy Bible, New Living Translation, copyright ©1996, 2004. Used by permission of Tyndale House Publishers, Inc., Wheaton IL 60189.

Scriptures marked KJV are taken from the King James Version of the Bible.

ISBN 978-1-58169-331-7
For Worldwide Distribution
Printed in the U.S.A.

RevPress
An imprint of Evergreen Press
P.O. Box 191540 • Mobile, AL 36619
800-367-8203

*Note: some names have been changed
to protect the privacy of the individuals mentioned.*

Author photo by Creative Photography, Abilene Texas

*To all the pastors and church leaders
who have been courageous and willing enough
to take off your own capes, masks, and protective shields
so that you may be vulnerable before others
as you walk side by side with the broken,
the rejected, and the forgotten...*

*To those of you who are victims of injustice
and those whose lives have been forever changed
by the consequences of violence...*

*To those who have heard the news and know
the tragic stories all too well and, because of it,
have chosen to get actively involved
in your churches and communities
to share the love of Christ
with all of humanity...*

*To those of you whose stories have become intertwined
with our own as we strive to live out God's calling,
we are honored and blessed to stand beside you
in the fight against injustice.
We dedicate this book
to all of you.*

*To God be the glory for all
He will accomplish!*

Table of Contents

1. Servants or Superstars? — 1
2. Leggo My Ego! — 7
3. To Know 'Em Is To Love 'Em — 29
4. Wanted: Demolition Crew — 43
5. Losin' Our Religion! — 57
6. What's the Difference? — 81
7. Ouch! I Though It Wasn't Supposed To Hurt! — 95
8. Rollercoaster! Rollercoaster! — 126
9. Running Into "Happily Ever After" — 153

Acknowledgments

First and foremost, I want to thank my Lord and Savior, Jesus Christ. Without You, I am meaningless and eternally hopeless.

I cannot thank my beautiful wife, Ashley, enough. Without your unconditional love, amazing patience, unlimited forgiveness, and endless support, this project would have never come to completion. Nor would I have the happiness I have today.

Special thanks also goes to…

My little princess, Alexis. You bring joy to my life that I never have experienced. You have taught me more about Christ's love for humanity more than any textbook, lecture, or pastor ever could.

My wonderful parents, Jeff and Katta Mitchell. You have always been by my side through my struggles, triumphs, and defeats. Without your unconditional love and support, there is absolutely no way I would be the person I am today.

Sheri Bennett. Without your tireless labor, indescribable devotion, and unconventional passion, there is absolutely no way that this book would have come into existence.

Justin Leifeste. Your art and passion to worship Jesus through art is breathtaking. Thank you for adding creativity and uniqueness to *The Superman Syndrome* through your illustrations.

My elders at Mission Abilene. You guys are incredible. Your support and confidence to trust the voice of God liberates me to pursue the heart of the Father without hindrance.

My staff. Your dedication, loyalty, and passion both to Jesus and humanity inspires me to be not only a better leader but also a better believer.

To the members of Mission Abilene. You guys are the greatest. It is an honor to lead such a supportive, energetic, and loving community of people.

Pastor Trace Michaels, Bishop Rob Nichols, Dr. Kelvin Kelley, and Dr. Tom Copeland. The countless hours of dialogue, the unconditional love and support, and the genuine integrity that each one of you has displayed to me throughout the years leaves me speechless. Without your guidance, counsel, and willingness to listen, my journey in ministry would have self-destructed years ago.

The RevPress staff—Brian, Jeff, and Kathy. Without your intense labor and incredible support, *The Superman Syndrome* would still only remain a personal dream.

And lastly, to all my friends. Thank you for being there to walk with me in the midst of struggles, to celebrate my times of success, and support me in my defeats. Without each one of you, my life would be consumed with loneliness and lack of zeal.

Live to Love,
Chad Mitchell

Like Chad, my utmost gratitude belongs to You, Jesus, the Lover and Healer of my soul. As Paul said, You truly are before all things and in You all things hold together—including every word we will ever write.

Chad, I can't even express what it has meant to me to be given the honor of being a part of this adventure, and what a journey it has been! You have pushed and shoved, inspired and encouraged, and never failed to speak the truth in love to me. You have exemplified and taught me tremendous strength through grace. You are still the only person I know who is as stubborn as I am! I can never thank you enough for letting God use you to reach me.

Tom and Lori Copeland, you have given me far more grace, love, and acceptance than I deserve. Tom, you gave me back the courage to live and to dream through your wise counsel. My journey back to life began with you. Lori, you inspired the passion and purpose in me to pursue a ministry called HOPE. Together, you both have shown me that there is true beauty in grace. Thank you for encouraging me and never giving up on me.

Mission Abilene, you have truly become my family in every sense—and what a colorful and wonderfully offbeat family you are! I love you. You've given me joy, peace, and belonging among you—not to mention some awesome stories! I am so blessed and grateful to call you my brothers and sisters in Christ.

And finally, my beautiful, beautiful children—Brittany, Mikey and Kaci, Andy, Elias, and Zachary—you are my life and my legacy. Thank you for loving me through struggles, misunderstandings, and separation. Thank you for your patience and forgiveness, and the room to grow and change. I pray that you can see in me and know the God of grace that I live and share today.

Be Blessed!
Sheri Bennett

Foreword

Truth. Big word. We are living and ministering in a world that believes there is no such thing as absolute truth. Those thoughts permeate throughout our culture and, sadly, our churches. Recently, I was studying the book of Ruth and was reminded of the story's setting: "in the days when the judges ruled" (Ruth 1:1 ESV). As I tried to imagine what that world would look like, the final words of the book of Judges rang in my head, "in those days there was no king in Israel. Everyone did what was right in his own eyes" (Judges 21:25 ESV). I thought, "Wow, what a horrible time to be alive!" and then I realized we are living in the same sort of days. Everyone is doing what is right in their own eyes! Truth today has taken on an entirely different meaning. Many of those we are ministering to doubt the existence of absolute truth. The reality is they believe that their truth is truth. Whatever they think, feel, or believe about something is truth to them, including the Bible.

The worst part is that there are pastors who are innocently beginning to bend on truth in their ministries due to a lack of focus from the King of kings to peripheral items that are not making a bit of difference for the kingdom. We are driven to look the part in every way and to have what we believe will bring in the people. The question is: What are we sacrificing for this? We are trying to do it all: big buildings, bright lights, snappy music, and slick campaigns. There is nothing inherently wrong with those things except that other things are taking the back seat such as prayer, study, and biblical truth on Sundays.

Have we become so busy running our churches that we have forgotten the Truth? Are we contemplative at all or are we too busy? We shake our heads when we think of those in this culture that are beginning to pass on truth, all the while allowing them to creep in and take control of our churches. We are contributing to the putrid relativism of our time! That is why the book you hold in your hand is so refreshing. It is nothing but truth. As I read through it, I found myself cut to the core many times. I needed to hear some of the things Chad has written here, as I often think that I am the modern day church Superman. I had to deal with a lot of issues during my time on these pages. And you know what, it was great! I am fortunate to have many friends that are pastors, evangelists, educators, and missionaries. I love them all dearly but shudder to think how many of us sweep things under the rug.

Chad Mitchell has exposed his heart for the Lord and for people in a very powerful way. We do think we can do it all. We want to do it all. We want to make a difference for Jesus. But we sometimes get so busy trying to do it all that we lose focus on the one thing that truly matters—Jesus and His love. What are we trying to do, build our kingdom or His? My friend has exposed himself and his ministry in unbelievable ways in the following pages, and I pray that you read this as I did—prayerfully ask the Lord to show you ways to move your ministry back toward truth, not your truth, but the truth found in the Scriptures and at the Cross. We have all done what this books speaks of. The question is, will we be open to change or continue trying to be Supermen? Thanks, Chad, for sharing truth and love. Thanks for ripping back the false façade that surrounds so many of us today. Thanks for reminding us of the real Truth and for making us take an inventory of our lives and ministries.

Don't put this book down until you have allowed it to absorb into your ministry. Buy a copy and give it to your best friend in ministry. May these words start a revolution for the One who gave His life for us. Let's allow these words to change our focus from ourselves back to Alpha and Omega. I pray you are blessed by these life changing pages.

Trace Michaels, Pastor,
South Pointe Church, Abilene, Texas

Introduction

First and foremost, my intention is to inspire and challenge fellow Christian leaders to dare to be the leaders God has called us to be, developing a ministry identity and style that reaches the unique needs of those within our individual spheres of influence. It is my prayer that this book will rekindle each leader's passion and desire to seek the true heart of Christ as they, in turn, challenge those within their reach.

Second, this book exposes the average American church member's common misconception that it is the sole responsibility of church leaders or the pastor to share the gospel. Regardless if we want to admit it or not, God ushers each one of us into place of leadership the very moment that we choose to accept Jesus Christ as our Savior. In Romans 10:14-15 (NLT), Paul explains:

> *But how can they call on him to save them unless they believe in him? And how can they believe in him if they have never heard about him? And how can they hear about him unless someone tells them? And how will anyone go and tell them without being sent? That is why the Scriptures say, "How beautiful are the feet of messengers who bring Good News!"*

In all of His infinite wisdom, God could have selected any vehicle possible to share the message of His gospel. But He didn't, He chose mankind to be His spokesman—to share our own personal salvation experience with others who don't know Him. Once we have encountered the Christ of the Cross and we believe the miracle and victory of His resurrection, we are chosen to share the redemption story with others. He saves us and in turn, we are called to tell others. But He didn't suddenly give us superhuman powers to save them ourselves. That's not our job. He calls us to use our own unique abilities—and yes, our weaknesses also—to offer the rest of humanity the opportunity to accept the same saving grace we have so freely received. We speak; He saves. You see, we didn't "choose" a career: He chose us to be His hands, His feet, and His voice! In that order: He calls us; we answer and obey.

Chapter 1

Servants or Superstars?

BEYOND AMBITION TO SERVANTHOOD

As a little boy, I practically idolized him. Who didn't? Who wouldn't want to be Superman? He is an American cultural icon that has fascinated scholars and critics alike as they explore the character's impact on individuals and society as a whole. When I was a kid, my Saturday mornings were booked solid—you got it!—right in my living room in front of the television set, living my life and my dreams of glory through cartoon after cartoon. Superman was one of my favorites.

One memorable Saturday, I had an epiphany—I decided I could BE Superman! I ran to my room and donned my Superman cape, which I was sure possessed superpowers. I climbed to the highest point of our living room couch, ready to make my debut. I was going to fly like Superman. With knees trembling in fear, I trusted my powers and heroically jumped. Up and away! (Okay, so I wasn't always the brightest crayon in the box!)

The Superman Syndrome

In midair, I realized my Superman cape was no contest for gravity. In a blink of an eye, I was lying facedown on the floor in terrible pain. The cartoon echoed in the background, "It's a bird! It's a plane! It's SUPERMAN!" and I tragically realized that he wasn't me! Hours later when I finally admitted to my parents how badly I was hurt, we discovered I had a broken collarbone. I learned a hard lesson that day: there was only one Superman, and I wasn't him! I simply needed to be who I was supposed to be and not someone else.

Sadly enough, this is the same reality for many church leaders. We read, we observe, and we research what is fueling other leaders and their churches—the reasons why they are growing. Then we try to mass-produce the formula that worked for them. We become generic plastic clones of someone else's convictions and inspirations. It took me a while but I finally realized that there is only one Billy Graham and I wasn't him. There is only one Martin Luther King, Jr. and I'm obviously not him either. I am and only can be Chad Mitchell, but I wasn't becoming the Chad Mitchell that Christ created me to be.

Please don't misunderstand me; I wholeheartedly believe that every Christian should have role models to inspire and encourage them—that "cloud of witnesses" spoken about in Hebrews. But if all I do is copycat another person or idea, I myself will become purposeless—empty and burned out as a result of not pursuing my own unique gifts. I can't do another person's job. I can only do what God has uniquely called me to do. No matter what role we carry in ministry, we are all designed and created for a special purpose—a purpose no one else can fulfill. One is no less and no greater than the other because it takes all of us to fulfill God's plan. Through nothing less than the inspiration of the Holy Spirit, Paul clarifies God's plan in practical terms to which we can all relate:

Servants or Superstars?

But our bodies have many parts, and God has put each part just where he wants it. How strange a body would be if it had only one part! Yes, there are many parts, but only one body. The eye can never say to the hand, "I don't need you." The head can't say to the feet, "I don't need you" (1 Cor. 12:18-21 NLT).

In the verses above, Paul vividly confirms that each one of us has an exclusive part to play in the greatest story ever written: the redemption of man through the sacrifice of Christ Jesus. As pastors, leaders, and even laymen, we make up the church: the body of Christ. A pastor alone is not the whole church. Just as the eye cannot do the hand's job, I cannot do Francis Chan's job. God has placed him in Simi Valley, California, to minister and serve in ways that I can't serve in Abilene, Texas. I respect and admire his ministry and outreach. I can gain insight into ministry by learning from him, but I can't be him. My church can't and shouldn't be his church. God's purpose for me within my church is exclusive only to me, and if I try to be Chan or Graham or Osteen, I will fall to the ground broken just as I did when I tried to be Superman.

As I've studied spiritual growth both individually and within the church over the years, one very glaring and apparent truth proves itself time and time again—churches grow and thrive simply because God is alive and present working in the lives of the leaders and the church body. The methods and formulas only work when we let God use us as leaders and pastors to meet specific needs and goals within our individual ministries. We are uniquely created, each one of us designed for a special purpose.

When I first became a pastor, I would read everything I could concerning church growth, the new worship trends, failsafe outreach methods, as well as all of the megachurch/superstar pastor success stories. Wouldn't it be so much easier if there were a guaranteed method to make our churches grow? Wouldn't we all want our church to grow like Joel Osteen's Lakewood Church in Houston? Or do we really? Over time, I finally realized that there is no single growth prescription that works in all cases and cultures. I was quickly becoming so consumed with modeling other pastors and churches, I began to morph into someone who was not genuine—a cheap imitation of whom God intended. I had to come to the realization that the assembly line of mass production had to cease, that God created me with unique abilities to impact my sphere of influence. I finally realized that for me to be the pastor and the man God wants me to be, I have to empty myself of all my superhero notions and megachurch ideas so the Holy Spirit can work in me and through me fulfilling the unique purpose God has for me.

How often we look at someone else's success and fame and we become less content with our own ministry. If I forget even for a season that my church is the Body of Christ, not the body of Chad or the coolest pastor I most recently read about, I will get trapped in the "Superman Syndrome," trying to do ministry on my terms, not His. Have you found yourself in that position yet? We want so much to be effective in ministry that we become so full of ideas and visions—our own as well as the latest greatest church leaders—that we lose sight of the fact that we are His servants, not His superstars. All that we do must point to Him and only Him. Many of us remember one of the contestants from the sixth season of American Idol, Chris Sligh. He risked his fame and fortune as the next American Idol to fulfill God's unique purpose, and though he came in tenth place that season, he shared the message of grace and salvation through his performances. While on tour with the American Idol, he wrote a hit single, "Empty Me" that exemplifies the need to get rid of ambitions and foolishness that we often disguise as ministry.

Servants or Superstars?

God has called us to share the gospel of Christ, not the gospel of the next best thing. All the greatest schemes and lofty visions of other pastors and other churches will not make my church, Mission Abilene, just like Lakewood Church nor should I want that for my church. My calling is to be right where I am, sharing the love and grace of Jesus Christ through exercising my own unique God-given abilities. No one else's step-by-step ministry plan can embellish what God has called me to do. He gave me only one model to follow that doesn't really have anything to do with worship style, the size of the church building, or the clothes we wear. There is only one true way to be Christian—to live out the name and to be like Jesus Christ. I don't need a secret formula or superhuman powers; I just have to commit to love and to live as He did—an extraordinary life.

As each one of us begins to contemplate God's inimitable purpose for ourselves as individuals and leaders, I pray that we first of all set aside all our ambitions. Let's rid ourselves of what we want and let the Spirit fill us with the desire and the determination to fulfill His plan. As I share my story and insights, our goal is not that you would copy my ministry style or for me to lay out step-by-step explicit instructions for you to follow to the letter, but rather for you to use my experiences to discover how to make your lives and your ministry fulfilled according to God's divine design. As we lead and minister in our churches, our families, and our communities, I hope that each one of us can daily pray the same words that Chris prayed and sang in his fifteen minutes of fame. Isn't it funny that although he lost and didn't live out his own dream as the next "American Idol," he still won in God's purpose and plan? The echoes of his heart and his ministry still ring true. As I share my heart with you, my prayer is that I will allow God to do the same for me, "Lord, please empty me."

The Superman Syndrome

STUDY QUESTIONS

1. Who was one of your childhood idols?

_____
_____
_____

2. Describe a time in your life when you looked at someone else's success and fame and became less content with your own ministry.

_____
_____
_____

3. What steps are you taking within your own ministry to point people to Jesus instead of at yourself?

_____
_____
_____

4. In what ways are you attempting to rid yourself of what you want and let the Spirit fill you with the desire and the determination to fulfill His plan?

_____
_____
_____

Chapter 2

Leggo My Ego!

BEYOND THE SPOTLIGHT TO GOD'S GLORY

Have you ever walked up to someone you recognized and assumed that they would know you too? They might stumble around trying to pretend they know you, but it's obvious to you both that they really don't have a clue who you are! It makes you seem small and insignificant somehow. You knock yourself off your own pedestal by assuming that you impress people and then find out you don't.

At times like these, you really wish you could just hit the rewind button and go back a few frames so you can undo your embarrassment. Instead of making a fool of yourself, just go on your merry way as if you had never seen that person. Solomon once said, "It is not good to eat too much honey, nor is it honorable to seek one's own honor" (Prov. 25:27 NIV).

All too often in this short life, I have found myself with my greedy paw stuck in the honey jar, seeking what I want, taking all the glory for myself. The only thing worse than being a copycat is thinking I'm important. As much as I hate to admit it, there was a time when my ministry was all about me and my agenda. I am called to share the Word of God not the word of Chad. But then God, in His own inimitable style, showed up and gifted me with a humbling experience. Recognition and respect is all too sweet! Though we are called to be humble as servants of Christ, it is all too easy for Christian pastors and leaders such as me to get stuck in the ego trap because of what we think we have accomplished.

Who Da Man?

I flew back from a huge speaking event in rural Alabama to speak at a small town revival in Winters, Texas. I was still feeling the rush of speaking to hundreds when I walked into a small church with only about fifty people in the pews. My swelled ego and I barely fit through the door together!

When I saw such a meager bunch, I contemplated whether this revival was worth my time. I wanted to leave. How could I speak here in this podunk revival when I had just spoken to more than 700 people? Hundreds—no, masses—heard me speak in Alabama so I would just be wasting my breath here. Most of these guys were probably already saved! What difference could I make in just a handful of people? Oops, there I go! Just like Winnie the Pooh, I got my egotistical head stuck in an empty honey jar!

A buddy of mine—obviously much humbler than me—was leading the worship at this same revival. His ego evidently fit through the door just fine, so he managed to persuade me to stay. Looking back, I have to wonder what he must have been thinking when he had to convince me that sharing the gospel with the masses or with just a few were both worth my time. I stayed and fulfilled my commitment. I preached and in spite of my ego, God still showed up. In fact, I will never forget that particular altar experience. God gave me the honor—no matter how undeserved—of seeing what He could do among a handful of people. More than twenty-five people gave their lives to the Lord that night—more than half the audience! I witnessed a greater movement of the Holy Spirit in that small half-empty sanctuary than I saw in the packed auditorium in Alabama. When God has a point to make, He hits hard! As tears streamed down my face that night, I suddenly realized that the gospel is not about me—it is all about Him. Somehow I had gotten so caught up in my own glory and fame that I thought somehow God expected me to change the world and that I would accomplish that through my own charisma and fame. I decided that He *needed* me and I was all important to growing His kingdom. My ego and self-satisfaction rested on a higher pedestal than God's own glory.

The next day, I bought a new Bible at a local Christian bookstore. I had it engraved with a constant reminder of His glory and my first lesson off the pedestal. "IT'S NOT ABOUT ME" was imprinted where my own name would normally have been, serving as a daily memo that God doesn't need me—He wants me.

Not to us, O Lord, not to us but to your name be the glory, because of your love and faithfulness (Psalm 115:1 NIV).

JESUS INCOGNITO

Jesus performed miraculous deeds and shared a message that was very controversial compared to the strict religious leaders of the day. His message was full of grace and mercy, offering forgiveness to anyone who would receive it, but He didn't wear fancy robes or boast so loudly of all His devoutness and perfection. He was known for His goodness and His gospel of grace, but He was just an ordinary-looking person. People expected Him to look extraordinary. Even to those who had often seen Him and heard Him preach, He was just another stranger in the midst of a crowd when He wasn't speaking or performing miracles. Sometimes even those who walked and talked with Him every day—those who should have readily known Him by sight—didn't even recognize Him.

After the crucifixion, Mary Magdalene stood crying outside His tomb. Jesus had been crucified three days earlier, and she had come to pay homage at His grave and anoint His body with scents and oils. When she arrived, the stone had been rolled away. His body was not there! She ran to tell John and Peter. They went inside the empty tomb, and suddenly they understood all that Jesus had been trying to tell them. They believed His resurrection and ran back to tell the others, leaving Mary behind. She didn't understand. In tears, she looked up. Two angels sat inside the tomb where Jesus would have been. Seeing her tears, they asked her, "Woman, why are you crying?"

She answered, "They have taken my Lord away and I don't know where they have taken Him!" Then she did something I consider very strange. She turned away! I don't know about any of you, but if I had just spoken to angels inside a tomb, I don't think I would have turned my back on them!

Torment took over her thoughts. *Hadn't those people done enough? Why had they stolen His dead body?* Blinded by her grief as she turned away from the tomb, she saw a gardener standing there. She didn't recognize him. He asked her, "Woman, why are you crying? Who are you looking for?"

He didn't sound familiar. She was so overwhelmed and desperate, she pleaded, "Sir, if you took Him away, please tell me where and I will get Him."

The next word changed everything. He simply spoke her name, "Mary!" It must have seemed to her that time had stopped as all of her inner turmoil and confusion came into focus. The grief that had blinded her was suddenly stripped away when she recognized Him. She cried out, "Rabboni!" It was Jesus (see John 20:11-16).

Expect Him

How often does Jesus show up and we fail to recognize Him because, like grief-stricken Mary, we are consumed with ourselves? Isn't it ironic that Jesus' own disciples were so consumed with fear of their own imprisonment, they hid and missed the resurrection? Leadership and ministry is often a lonely business. And when we are consumed with ourselves, we find that we are lonelier still. When we desire to be known by our own merit rather than by what He has done within us, we aren't seeking Him or expecting Him. When ministry is about me, I tend to spend less time with Him. Before I realize it, my ministry begins to weaken and fail. I can't do this job on my own. In John 15:5 Jesus warns us,

> *I am the vine; you are the branches. Those who remain in me, and I in them, will produce much fruit. For **apart from me you can do nothing*** (NLT, emphasis added).

We are not effective in ministry without Him. We must seek Him and make Him known.

After Jesus' death, the disciples were frozen in fear. He had told them that they would not be alone, but they didn't believe Him. They had walked and talked with Him every day. He had given explicit details of what was to come, but they did not understand. I would think that if Jesus had told me He would rise up in three days, I would be there watching and expecting a miracle. Or would I?

Mary Magdalene was the first person to go to Jesus' grave to honor Him in death, and the first person to see Him after His resurrection. And even she didn't recognize Him when she first saw Him. She thought He was a lowly gardener—no one special! Mary knew Jesus far too well to have such a close encounter and not remember His face. He had literally delivered her from demons and accepted her in her madness. She followed Him and served His every need as He spread His message, yet she didn't know Him. I find that almost unbelievable, yet do I recognize Him when He shows up in my everyday walk?

If Jesus had been as egocentric as most of us, He may have taken great offense at Mary's forgetfulness. But Jesus wasn't all about His own glory. He was even put to the test again that very same day. On the road to Emmaus, two disciples were deep in conversation. They had seen and heard all the events of the last three days but still had not comprehended that Jesus was really alive and that His resurrection was history in the making and would literally change the world. They were so preoccupied with their own thoughts and lost hopes that they failed to recognize Jesus when He joined them. Before the crucifixion, they were certain He was the expected Messiah and would save the world, but it was all forgotten at His death. Jesus' voice didn't register, "What are you guys talking about and why are you so sad?"

In disbelief, Cleopas asked, "Are you a stranger? Have you not heard the news about Jesus?" They tried to explain but they were so confused themselves, their answers just made them need to ask more questions! But Jesus fully understood and chastised them for their unbelief in all that He had promised, yet they still didn't realize they were talking to the very Jesus they were discussing! They invited this curious stranger to supper. It was not until He broke the bread and blessed it that they finally opened their eyes and realized who He was. And then He was gone (see Luke 24:13-31).

Twice in the most fateful day in history and in eternity, people who loved Him and followed Him were so distracted they didn't even know Him—their Messiah, their Savior, their intimate Friend. Caught up in their dismay and sorrow, none of them were even looking for Jesus and definitely not expecting Him. But He still showed up. Were His feelings hurt? Did He curse them? No, He was much more interested in His real purpose: to show them His Daddy's glory—the glory of One who created all things and held the universe in the palm of His hand. Jesus was a King in every sense, yet He considered Himself a servant to the God of heaven and earth.

My heart pounds as the realization of the truth hits me between the eyes. How often am I so preoccupied or consumed with my own agenda that I don't even know Him when He shows up? If not for the persuasion of a more humble worship leader, I would have missed Him altogether that fateful night in Winters, Texas. He showed up and His presence changed my life and the lives of the twenty-five people who committed their hearts to Him.

When I'm so consumed with my own acclaim, my own needs and my desires, I don't look for Him. Sometimes as ministry leaders and teachers, we just go through the motions in order to do the "job" of ministry. I'm so busy putting myself out there for everyone to see that I don't even expect Him to show up. It gets so lonely up there on the podium by myself. Instead of inviting Him and expecting Him, I'm showing up in His place! If I focus only on His purpose and His glory, I seek only Him. The words of His teaching prayer take on a much deeper meaning:

*And do not lead us into temptation, but deliver us from evil. For **Yours** is the kingdom and the power and the glory forever. Amen* (Matt. 6:13 NASB, emphasis added).

LIGHTS! CAMERA!...ATTITUDE!

In life and in leadership, it all comes down to attitude. If you are like me, many of you may battle your own ego-driven attitude. I'm so involved in my wants, my needs, my desires, that I don't have any room left for anyone else, least of all Christ! And every day I focus on me, the worse my attitude gets! Chuck Swindoll is well-known for saying,

> The longer I live, the more I realize the impact of attitude on life...The only thing we can do is play on the one string we have, and that is our attitude. I am convinced that life is 10% what happens to me and 90% of how I react to it. And so it is with you...We are in charge of our attitudes.

His words ring so true, but we let our attitudes take charge of us when we see ourselves as more important than we actually are. We like to take things in hand and be in control. We have lights! We have camera! All eyes on us! And with all that, boy do we have some attitude! We are often like our own children saying, "Look at me, Daddy! Look at me! See what I can do!"

Some of the greatest struggles throughout my life have been with my own attitude. How often I have to be the top dog in every situation—not just in front of a crowd. I've always had "Look at me! Look at me!" tendencies, but instead of showing off how smart or tough or wise I was, I proved how arrogant and ignorant I could be! All too often my sarcasm gets me in some sticky situations. An unchecked arrogant attitude never

Leggo My Ego!

leads anywhere but trouble, especially when my attitude meets its match. Hopefully, I'm outgrowing my less attractive attitudes but I've had to learn the hard way...

Like most college freshmen out in the adult world, I thought I was invincible and king of my own personal universe. No one could stop me and no one could put me down. Life was going my way simply because I willed it—or so I thought! I wanted to impress a girlfriend, so a buddy and I drove three and one-half hours to Dallas, Texas, to watch her play soccer on the university team. Though our alma mater didn't win that night, I proved myself a loyal and supportive boyfriend. Mission accomplished! Everything was great until we headed for home.

A few miles out of the Metroplex, I noticed that my steering wheel had become extremely hard to maneuver. I soon discovered that the power steering pump had gone on permanent strike. It was going to be a long ride home! If you've ever driven without power steering, you know this would be an effort for a musclebound athlete. I was just a tired fat kid with two or three more hours of driving ahead. What a workout! My perfect evening was quickly taking a downhill spiral.

About twenty miles from Abilene, my exhaustion and aggravation took over as I put the pedal to the metal in anticipation of home. And wouldn't you just know it? In a matter of minutes, twinkling red and blue lights appeared in my rearview mirror. With frustration mounting, I pulled over to the side of the road. A speeding ticket was not going to make my day! To make matters worse, I think I met up with Sheriff Buford T. Justice himself! The Texas state trooper swaggered up to my window decked out in shades and a gun holster riding low on his hips, "Sir, will you please step out of the truck?"

If only I had checked my arrogant attitude before I started talking. Instead, my mouth jumped into gear long before my brain did. With an impatient sigh, I rolled my eyes in argument, "What? I don't need to get out of the truck for you to give me a business card I'm going to have to pay for!"

Our battle of wills had just begun, and the officer didn't seem to think I was nearly as smart as I did. He ordered, "I said, get out of the car now!"

Mocking him, I complied, "Uh, yes Sir!"

Evidently my brain still wasn't in gear and my arrogant compliance didn't seem to impress him. "Son, I am going to write you a ticket for speeding, a ticket for no seatbelt, and a ticket for failure to use your turn signal."

Talk about overkill! Who did this guy think he was giving me all those tickets? Attitude! Who did I think I was to argue? You would think that the idea of my dwindling bank account would shut me up, but not a chance! I declared my indignation, "You have got to be kidding me! You might as well take me to jail—that will definitely help your quota."

He wasn't so amused. I thought I was somebody, but after all, he was the one with the badge. "Sir, turn around and put your hands behind your back."

The threat of handcuffs didn't even muzzle me as I tried to back my way out of this predicament, "Whoa! Wait just a minute! Can't you take a joke?"

God's good grace must have been hard at work because for some reason my Texas-friendly trooper found enough mercy to disregard my smart mouth and bad attitude. Instead of escorting me to my own private suite in the county's deluxe motel, he left me with his official calling card authorized by the state of Texas. His kindness would ultimately require my $400 donation to the local precinct and a great big chunk of my pride. Finally, making sure I understood that he had won this battle of wills, Officer Justice concluded our friendly little chat with a congenial "Have a nice day!"

Leggo My Ego!

As the flashing lights faded behind us, I steamed. My buddy who sat quietly in the car throughout the whole ordeal punched me in the shoulder and chided, "Nice attitude!"

I would not admit even to my friend that I got just exactly what I deserved, so I feigned ignorance, "What are you talking about?"

He went on, "Your attitude almost took you to jail!"

The truth stung and attitude reared its ugly head one more time. "Shut it!"

My encounter with the patrol officer grew from a funnel cloud to a tornado as his attitude clashed with my own. Attitude definitely made an impact here. Hmmm…90 percent how I react. If I had reacted a little more humbly, I have to wonder if he would have been a little more lenient without my 90 percent!

OUT OF THE SPOTLIGHT!

I engaged in a battle of egos with that police officer—a battle I couldn't win on my own. I practically dared him to take me down because I wanted to prove I was tough. The world perceives greatness as being the very best—the toughest, the prettiest, the smartest, the fastest, or the richest. We thrive on competition. We have this king-of-the-mountain mentality that says the one with the most wins all and is all. Our role models are those with the most power, the most money, the most awards, the most luxuries, and the most fame. We want what they have, and we want to be where they are. When we get to the top, we expect to be treated differently. After all, success merits more prestige, respect, and recognition than the average achiever, even in our desire to serve God more and to be more for His kingdom.

In our quest for the best, even we Christians sometimes lose sight of our own beginnings as humility takes a back seat. We tend to forget our original purpose as ego takes its place. This amnesia has afflicted the most prestigious leaders throughout the ages, even ancient kings and high priests. But Jesus Christ, just a lowly carpenter by trade, taught us a different way, redefining greatness and leadership. Jesus didn't seek the spotlight. In fact, He tried very hard to avoid it. He said,

> *Not so with you. Instead, whoever wants to become great among you must be your servant, and whoever wants to be first must be your slave—just as the Son of Man did not come to be served, but to serve, and to give his life as a ransom for many* (Matt. 20:26-28 NIV).

To be the greatest, I must be willing to be the least. We're back to square one again, aren't we? It's not about me! To be first, I must be last. Jesus' words constantly remind me that I am called to be a servant of all. Jesus Christ—my Redeemer, my Lord, and my Maker—came to earth to serve others, giving His very own life away. If I honestly call myself one of His disciples, then I must follow in His footsteps and do just as He did. I must love and serve others in spite of the cost.

Christ was a servant by nature. He had the heart of a servant—an innate compulsion and desire to love and give to others with His whole heart, never expecting anything in return. Serving was not what Jesus did but rather who He was. In giving His very own life to love and serve others, a carpenter became a king.

Okay, I can be a servant. I can love people. But somewhere along the way, we begin to gain merit by how much good we do. We compete in servanthood! Whoever is the best and busiest servant wins the prize. We still don't get it! Thomas Merton once told another monk: "Quit keeping score altogether and surrender yourself with all your sinfulness to God who sees neither the score nor the scorekeeper but only His child redeemed by Christ."

Let go of that ego! Following Jesus is not a competition but simply and humbly living out the grace that He has so freely given to us. Humility conflicts with the world's perception of greatness and denies ambition and conceit. We work so hard to climb to the top even in ministry, but true leadership and greatness means that our hearts remain at ground level always serving another.

Over the past ten years, I have learned that those who truly impact lives are those who lead by serving. But we can't just take on the attitude of servant—we must take on the attitude of *the* Servant, Jesus Christ. All lights and cameras are on Him, not us. When we have done all we can—when thinking of others first before ourselves becomes instinctive, then we have just begun to understand what it means to be a Christian.

THE GAME PLAN

We are called to serve wherever we are. Our mission may have a good purpose, but some of us can't get beyond grabbing kudos for our own achievements. It's virtually impossible to point to God's glory when we're pointing all the lights and cameras on us. Even Paul struggled with his own ego, but like a football coach, he gives us a game plan to go beyond our own glory and pass off the ball to the new quarterback, Abba Father, so He can make the score. We point to His glory rather than our own. Jesus wrote the playbook Himself by His example:

> *Your attitude should be the same as that of Christ Jesus: Who, being in very nature God, did not consider equality with God something to be grasped, but made himself nothing, taking the very nature of a servant, being made in*

human likeness. And being found in appearance as a man, he humbled himself and became obedient to death— even death on a cross! Therefore God exalted him to the highest place and gave him the name that is above every name, that at the name of Jesus every knee should bow, in heaven and on earth and under the earth, and every tongue confess that Jesus Christ is Lord, to the glory of God the Father (Phil. 2:5-11 NIV).

Paul doesn't waste his words. His revolutionary concept presents a whole new way of thinking and promotes an effective strategy to defeat our biggest rival—our ego. Some of us have wasted a lot of time, energy, and resources, building acclaimed reputations to gain a plastic trophy that will never last beyond this life. After all, we want to look good when we climb up on our self-made pedestal to receive our prize. And we knock down anyone or anything that gets in our way. "Look at me! Look at me! I'm good!" Oh, how we enjoy the spotlight! I remember the rush so well when I was speaking before hundreds in Alabama. Ego is a strong and mighty foe but he's just a one-man team. If we truly commit ourselves to victory, we don't hog the glory. To win, we have to walk out of the spotlight. We play as a team, and Christ Himself is our captain and star player.

Paul's main strategy is to move beyond our own self-seeking glory to take on the mind of Christ and evaluate our attitude. He said, "Your attitude should be the same as that of Christ Jesus." We strive so hard to be Jesus to the world, yet we can never quite make the touchdown before we get tackled! But maybe it's because we are looking through our eyes, not His. How easy it is to fall into the trap of thinking with our own minds rather than His. We give Him our hearts and He gives us a new mind—if we let Him. And when we ignore a couple of words out of Paul's strategy, it makes all the difference. Careful—Paul's words may sting a little!

We sometimes tend to think we know all we need to know to answer these kinds of questions—but sometimes our humble hearts can help us more than our proud minds. We never really know enough until we recognize that God alone knows it all (1 Cor. 8:2-3 MSG).

We vainly strive to be just like Jesus the way we see Him—as goodness, perfection, the Savior, Prince of Peace, King of Kings, and all things to all people. But that isn't what Paul said. He said to take on the attitude of Christ, not become Jesus, the Messiah—in other words, look at our own lives in the same way that Christ viewed Himself. It's a completely different image. We put Him on a pedestal, and it's an impossible height to climb; but Christ saw Himself as the servant of man. That brings Him a little more down to earth, doesn't it? Though He knew He was the King and the Son of God, He didn't present Himself that way. Rather than focusing on His lofty titles and position, He focused on His purpose, which pointed all glory to His Father.

Now Give It All Ya Got!

With a new attitude in mind, we are now ready to take action and play the game. We can't win the game if we don't put our new attitude out there on the playing field. In essence, we have to live out Christ's attitude, and it's nothing like we're used to! Paul explained very clearly how Jesus put His attitude in action: He "made Himself nothing, taking the very nature of a servant…" Ugh, servant! Where's the glory in that? But that is exactly the point—there is no glory. The attitude of Christ doesn't seek glory, only humility. When you've prided yourself on being the star quarterback in your own game of life, you might find it deflating to reduce yourself to become the waterboy! But that's exactly what Jesus did. We have to back up our attitude with action, just as He did.

Jesus is the real thing. He could have pulled a power trip and taken up His deserving role as King, but He knew the true source of that power came from His Father, so He took the lowest of all positions to elevate His Father. Jesus went over and beyond in obedience to God's plan when most of us are content with being good enough in our own actions. Paul encourages us to be obedient to our Savior as He was to His Father. "And being found in appearance as a man, He humbled Himself and became obedient to death—even death on a cross!" He gave His utmost, and we're okay with "That's good enough." At times in our work for the Lord, we aren't even obedient enough to inconvenience ourselves and pick up a person walking down the street—much less be obedient to the point of death!

True victory in this battle of ego is found in utter humility with nothing held back. The moment Jesus gave up His spirit on the cross, the sky darkened and the thunder rolled. To the crowd looking on, it must have seemed that all was lost and there was no way to win. Even Mary Magdalene, the disciples, and the men on the road to Emmaus had given up the battle because of death. They forgot that Jesus had told them the whole game plan! Three days later, much to their surprise, the game was indeed won through Jesus' resurrection, but He never could have made the winning score without His sacrifice.

Boomerang!

It all sounds good in theory. I think it's great that Paul so kindly shared his self-help tips on letting go of our ego, but

Leggo My Ego!

what good is it really if we follow that advice? I mean, really—death? Yet that's what God requires. Paul declares an amazing reward that we may receive in complete obedience through Christ's example. He died a criminal's death, but it didn't end there. Read Paul's words again:

> *Therefore God exalted him to the highest place and gave him the name that is above every name, that at the name of Jesus every knee should bow, in heaven and on earth and under the earth, and every tongue confess that Jesus Christ is Lord, to the glory of God the Father.*

A week before His death, multitudes praised His name and wanted to crown Him King. They shouted, "Hosanna to the King!" (Makes me remember my Alabama glory when everyone thought I was so wonderful!) Yet even then—unlike me—Jesus rode into town on a donkey rather than a stallion fit for a king! Several times within the week that followed, He had opportunity after opportunity to take up His crown if He had used His God-given power. Christ remained true to the game plan, trusting in the eternal victory. He gave up glory and honor in obedience, but God poured His own glory on Him in reward. He gave up an earthly kingdom to fulfill His mission, but God put Him back on the throne for eternity. Glory given and greater glory returned. Today and forever, Jesus is our King of Kings!

Jesus is the everlasting example of truth. If we choose to be as obedient as He was, we will receive His glory in heaven. Scripture proclaims, "Humble yourselves, therefore, under God's mighty hand, that he may lift you up in due time" (1 Peter 5:6 NIV). Whatever we do, we do it under God's mighty hand—under His direction. I don't know about you, but I would much rather be in obedience under Him. I may need that continual engraved reminder "It's not about you," but I think I can pass on this world's glory so that He will lift me up when my time comes.

God's glory is like a boomerang. We throw it up to Him and in His time, He returns it back to us. I reflect on my life lesson that night in little Winters, Texas, and how dramatically His truth has changed my life. I'm certainly not proud of who I was before, but I'm humbled by who I am now. And I'm learning that the change in me affected others even that very next day. I met Sheri when she was a sales associate at the local Christian bookstore. Our relationship was purely in customer service then. I may not have even realized that my egotistical attitude would have been noticed by others in such minimal circumstances, but little did I know that God had a plan for our friendship long before she ever walked in the doors of my church or I became her pastor. She commuted to work then from another town and had no idea that she would soon move to Abilene and eventually to the Mission. As she read my reflections on my Winters' revelation, she added her own. She emailed me her side of the story:

> I just realized something ironic but so awesome, and I never saw it until now...You told the story of the Alabama and Winters' revivals, and you came into the store to imprint your Bible the very next day with "It's Not About You." You had suddenly realized that the message you had to give didn't have anything to do with you but all to do with Christ instead. You kinda knocked yourself off your own pedestal.
>
> But you probably didn't realize your lesson taught me something that day too. You had come in the store several times with another pastor or on your own. And honestly, I really couldn't get a handle on you—I

Leggo My Ego!

thought you were kind of arrogant. I guess that's where the "young punk preacher wannabe" image came from. Now remember, I really didn't know you except in another pastor's shadow then. The only times I had ever seen you were in Bible Book Store. I hadn't even considered going to the Mission yet. You told me you wanted to imprint your Bible and you wanted it right then. I went to the back to do it. Usually, customers didn't go behind the counter, but you just barged right on through behind me to the imprint machine to watch. I remember thinking, "Geez, who does he think he is? He's going to stand there to watch to make sure I do it right!" And you just kept talking! You were making me nervous—you usually didn't talk so much! But as I worked (very worried I was going to screw it up with you watching, by the way) I started really listening. You told me that story and why you were imprinting that statement on your Bible as a reminder. I saw a completely different side of you. Your whole spirit was totally humble in light of God's significance. That was the day I realized that there was much more to you than met the eye. Your faith and your commitment went much deeper than your wannabe pastor image.

The irony is that you came into the store completely humbled…but your willingness to take your own ego out of your ministry to give God the glory is exactly that gave you credibility in my eyes. You weren't a prickly thistle anymore. You became the "monument" in Isaiah 55:12-13:

So you'll go out in joy, you'll be led into a whole and complete life. The mountains and hills will lead the parade, bursting with song. All the trees of the forest will join the procession, exuberant with applause. No more thistles, but giant sequoias, no more thornbushes, but stately pines—monuments to me, to God, living and lasting evidence of God (MSG).

Sometimes God is so gracious and good that He shares His glory on earth as we live and breathe. That day He gave me credibility as a pastor in the eyes of another. I didn't realize until years later that my story had impacted her at all. Neither Sheri nor I knew of God's plan that day. We barely knew each other so we had no idea of what He had in store. In the years that followed, I became not just her friend but her pastor. And I wonder if not for those few moments in that little store, would she have allowed God to lead her to the Mission or to accept me as her pastor? Her own healing began even in that very moment as God began to work within her.

AND HIS GLORY CONTINUES…

It's not about me and never has been. God showed up in that little church in Winters the night before, but His glory showed up that day in the back room of a bookstore. I'm nowhere near perfect, but God daily reminds me to give all the glory to Him—in every word I speak and every step I take. I strive to be a living example of His glory and to speak only Christ rather than myself.

Those who speak for themselves want glory only for themselves, but a person who seeks to honor the one who sent him speaks truth, not lies (John 7:18 NLT).

That night in that little church I almost missed God's presence. If I had walked out the door, I wouldn't have heard Him speak to me so clearly. But a tender voice intimately called my

Leggo My Ego!

name that night, just as He had called out to Mary Magdalene in the garden. As all those people came to the altar, He called my name, "Chad!" And I knew it was Him.

In the past few years, God has done such amazing things in my life and in my faith simply because I let go of my own ego and let Him work in me and through me. He has stretched me further than I could have imagined and carried me to heights I could never have climbed on my own. My spiritual life and my ministry have been blessed because of Him. I am absolutely nothing without Him. I am so glad that He took me off my pedestal in that West Texas church so that I can live and serve and love in His name and His name only. I am so humbly grateful that He still loves me and calls me by name.

Now all glory to God, who is able to keep you from falling away and will bring you with great joy into his glorious presence without a single fault (Jude 1:24 NLT).

STUDY QUESTIONS

1. Hindsight is more accurate than foresight. Look back objectively throughout your past ministry experiences. Have there been times when you have been so preoccupied or consumed with your own agenda that you failed to recognize the presence of Jesus?

_____
_____
_____

2. In your quest for the best, have you ever lost sight of your own beginnings as your humility took a backseat? Explain.

_____
_____
_____

3. Those who truly impact lives are those who lead by serving. How are you currently serving humanity outside of the spotlight?

_____
_____
_____

4. How are you striving to be a living example of His glory—speaking only Christ rather than yourself?

_____
_____
_____

5. In what ways do you need to let go of your ego and let Christ work in you and through you?

_____
_____
_____

Chapter 3

To Know 'Em Is To Love 'Em!

BEYOND ACQUAINTANCE TO RELATIONSHIP

Humility in serving: that's what God has called each one of us to do regardless if we are a church leader or a layperson. But it's more than serving nameless, faceless people. Jesus told us not only to serve but to love others as He loved us. In the busyness of ministry, we sometimes forget one of His greatest commandments. When we are blinded by the brightness of the spotlight, we don't really see or know those whom we serve.

I bumped into a young man in the hallway of my office building. I recognized him but couldn't remember his name. I hadn't seen him for years, but I was late for a meeting and in a hurry so I'd have to fake it. Have you ever done that? Rather than take the time to reach out to another even in our own place of ministry, we feign concern as we go on our way. I never even slowed down as I greeted him in passing, "Man, how's it going? Are you doing all right?"

I faintly heard him answer as I continued on my way, "Yeah, I'm doing all right."

"Well, good for you! Take it easy!" I called back over my shoulder. As I closed my office door, conviction fell heavy on my shoulders. Did I really care how the guy was doing? Would I have stopped and listened to him if he had said, "Man, my life sucks! I feel like nothin' is going my way!" Would I have made an excuse to meet my next appointment? Sometimes I believe God arranges divine appointments in the midst of our busyness so that we can be blessed and be a blessing, but His holy interruptions often go ignored because of our ministry agenda. How often I forget it isn't my ministry but His. I can't change that moment in the past, but I hope and pray that if the Holy Spirit schedules a divine appointment, I will set aside my calendar for His. When a similar situation happens again, I pray that I will stop, take the time to listen with full attention, and encourage, "God bless you. I want you to know I'm here for you. How can I help?"

Do I Walk the Talk?

None of us have "arrived." No matter how long it's been since we prayed the sinner's prayer, our salvation is ongoing. We fall down; we get back up. We fall down again, and we get back up again. Even now in this very moment, I am being saved as I share the message of the gospel with my church and community and you. I am not above you nor ahead of you—I'm walking with you. Long before I became the congregational pastor of Mission Abilene, I promised to walk with people through their struggles and addictions until they can stand on their own. It's an easy promise to make but sometimes not so easy to keep. It doesn't take much to talk the talk, but it takes commitment to walk it. I have learned that I can't just be acquainted with people—I have to get to know them. I have to be a living example of Christ's love through true friendship.

One of Scripture's best demonstrations of friendship is found in the story of the paralyzed man and his four buddies (see Mark 2:1-12). Jesus was staying at a friend's house in Capernaum. His radical teachings and His miracles were the talk of the town. News of His arrival spread like wildfire, and He drew a crowd as quickly as a schoolyard fight would. Come on, you remember how it was in middle school. One kid yelled "Fight!" and kids swarmed in from all directions, circling in so tight around the brawl that the teachers couldn't get in to break it up. Jesus wasn't throwing any punches—not physical ones anyway—but His crowd was no less intense.

"Jesus is preaching!" People swarmed in from every street and byway. In no time, the crowd had wedged in His host's home so tight that no one else could fit through the doors or windows. But four determined young men had a paraplegic friend who was in need of one of Jesus' miracles, and they weren't going to let this mob hold them back. They took extreme measures that would probably get them arrested today. They hoisted their friend on a makeshift stretcher to the top of the house and cut a hole in the roof. Remember, this was another man's home! Can you imagine what the homeowner must have been thinking when dirt started falling on his head? It took some nerve for those four guys to rip out another man's roof just so their buddy could meet Jesus.

Then they lowered their friend on his stretcher right in front of Jesus. The Savior looked up through the roof and saw the four men looking down on Jesus and their friend, fully expecting Him to make the lame man walk. He was impressed by their boldness and faith. He turned to the lame man, "Son, your sins are forgiven!" His unexpected words caused a buzz among the crowd. Then Jesus told the forgiven man, "Take your mat and go home." The healed man stood up, picked up his mat as the stunned crowd opened a pathway, and he walked out the door. I can only imagine the "high fives" taking place on top of the roof!

What a beautiful example of true friendship! These men didn't just wish their friend better. They didn't just talk about who Jesus was or what He could do. They took action and did what he couldn't do on his own. They carried him into the presence of the Lord. He was not only healed—he was also forgiven. His life was forever changed.

As a young minister, I was taught how to hand out tracts, give away Bibles, and pray for people. All that is well and good, but time and time again, I found myself asking, "Is this all God wants us to do?" Think about it. We proclaim to be "fishers of men," but what do we do with them after we catch them? We get them to church, save them, baptize them, and clean them up, but when they are finally "good to go," we abandon them as we become complacent in our commitment to walk with them.

Fishing for bass may be a sport, but fishing for men is not—Christ never intended discipleship to be a "catch and release" program. Even within the church, we sometimes forget that salvation is *not* a one-time experience: we are saved and we are being saved continually—even the pastors and leaders! Jesus wants our salvation to go beyond simple acquaintance with the gospel, and discipleship to go beyond simple acquaintance with people. He expects both to become a way of life.

My deep friendship with the Lord and the friendships I have developed through my life and ministry have been the roots of strength that have brought me to where I am today. If I had never gone beyond my introduction to Christ and His message or the people who led me to Him, I would definitely need to question my motives in ministry and their motives in friendship. The salvation experience is the foundational blessing of all blessings, but it is an evolutionary process.

> *For the message of the cross is foolishness to those who are headed for destruction, but we who are being saved know it is the very power of God* (1 Cor. 1:18 NLT).

In my church, we strive to keep my original promise: to walk with people when life is good and we see God working, but also to walk with them when life is messed up and seemingly hopeless. We don't give up; we keep walking with each other through the ups and downs in faith. We have journeyed alongside addicts and alcoholics, gang members, convicts, the homeless, and the rejects of society. Sometimes it's easy to walk together, and sometimes we have to push people along or hold each other accountable when we fight against God's will. But His glory is revealed in lives that are forever changed by the love and grace of Jesus Christ.

Do I Look and Smell Like Jesus?

So how do I make a difference? Have you ever wondered what a different world we would live in if each one of us took the time to truly listen and care about the people we encounter on a daily basis? There's an old 70s chorus that says, "They will know we are Christians by our love." Do the people you see every day know who and what you are by the way you treat them? Or do you have to tell them? When they say, "He's a Christian," do they say it in awe of the Christ they see in you, or do they sniff with disdain at the stench of a hypocrite? If that guy at work, whom everyone thinks is a jerk, sees the love of Christ in you, maybe he would confess that his marriage is falling apart and he's hurting. Just maybe he is in desperate need for someone to listen. What if you were a friend to everyday strangers like the bum who stands on that busy corner you pass every day on your way to work? His handwritten cardboard sign reads, "Homeless and hungry—will work for food." Instead of thinking, *Get a job!* when you pass by, what if you take him to get an Egg McMuffin and learn that he suffers from post-traumatic stress disorder since he witnessed his own wife's decapitation in a car wreck? You might begin to understand that the trauma and guilt keeps him so stuck in an unchangeable moment of the past that he clings to a bottle because he can't handle the memory or everyday stress of life. His choices cripple him and force him to live on the streets. If you knew, would you keep passing by him every day?

Maybe if we recognized the struggles of even a few of the countless people we see every day, we would reach out a hand to offer hope rather than pretend not to see, or worse yet, not even notice their need. What would change if we extended our friendship beyond small-time change, empty words, and half-hearted promises to pray for them? In order to look like Jesus, we have to "see" like Jesus. We have to meet people at their need. I wonder how many of us can say that we live out Paul's proclamation:

> *But thanks be to God, who always leads us in triumphal procession in Christ and through us spreads everywhere the fragrance of the knowledge of him. For we are to God* ***the aroma of Christ among those who are being saved and those who are perishing****. To the one we are the smell of death; to the other, the fragrance of life. And who is equal to such a task? Unlike so many, we do not peddle the word of God for profit. On the contrary, in Christ we speak before*

To Know 'Em Is To Love 'Em

God with sincerity, like men sent from God (2 Cor. 2:14-17 NIV, emphasis added).

In 2007, the nation was horrified as the story unraveled about a young man, Cho Seung-Hui, who massacred thirty-two people and killed himself in the Virginia Tech campus shooting. "He Was a Loner" was emblazoned across the headlines. In the aftermath of the shooting, politicians and Christians cried out about the evil and hatred within this young man and others like him. I wonder if it would have made a difference if someone had taken the time to listen in earnest and really get to know Cho when he was a young immigrant boy, long before he acquired a killer's mentality. Instead of condemnation, maybe we should consider the hurt and anguish that drove him to such desperation and hate. People said that they had reached out to him, but had they reached out with more than words? I don't know what measures people took to love Cho, but I do know that sometimes we do a lot of talking and then fall short of living it out.

So the question remains: Do we look and smell like Christians? When our actions don't reflect our words, we exude the stench of death and judgment rather than emanate the fragrance of life through unconditional love and mercy. I wonder if anyone reached out to Cho in the same radical grace Christ offered to the lepers, the bleeding woman, the adulteress, and even the thieves who hung on either side of Him on Mt. Calvary. I wonder if I would have, as a pastor and a friend. To show others who Christ is, we have to be willing to love the unlovable and be aware enough to notice the unnoticeable right where they are. Suppose if someone would not only have told Cho about the love of Christ but also lived as a paradigm to His love through their everyday actions and attitudes. I can't guarantee that Cho's life would have changed, but the possibility for change would have been present.

If nowhere else, people should be able to find refuge in the body of Christ. Our whole purpose is to love as Jesus loved so that the mystery of the gospel will be made known and lives will be changed. Christ within us is the "hope of glory" (Col. 1:27 NIV) for ourselves and for others. Do I stink or am I a sweet aroma?

Ravi Zacharias, in his book *Cries of the Heart: Bringing God Near When He Feels So Far*, said,

> The church ought to be a place of inner healing and restoration. Here the patience of Christ and the wisdom of a disciplined life is needed to instruct and guide. When a person stumbles or is taken in sin, it is the privileged call of the church of Christ to reach out and to help restore. When one struggles with feelings that God is so far away, the arms of those who are part of the church will be the only arms God has to draw such people near. When someone feels abandoned, the hearts of the people of God may be the only hearts God can tap to feel with this person.

DO I LOVE LIKE JESUS?

We were created for relationship with God and with others. The original Adam lived in paradise where everything was perfect and he wanted for nothing, yet God still saw that he was lonely. So He created Eve to be a partner and a companion—a friend. So if Adam needed a friend in God's made-to-order garden of Eden, don't you think we all need friends in today's messed-up, imperfect world?

To Know 'Em Is To Love 'Em

As Christian leaders, we think we have this "love thy neighbor" concept down pat! We shake a few hands, we meet and greet a few visitors on Sundays, and we promise to pray for others through the week. We might even build or serve in community ministries such as food and clothing pantries, raise money for benevolence funds, or organize support and recovery ministries. In obedience to Christ's mandate, we go about the business of loving our neighbors as ourselves. All of these things are great and should be part of the ministry of any church. But is it enough? I have to ask myself: Am I a friend to others in the sense that Jesus was a friend to His disciples and others who followed Him? Am I willing to go above and beyond the call of duty? In essence, do I love like Jesus?

I have made a lifetime commitment to live to love. Loving others is a response to Christ's unconditional love for me. If He could love me at my worst, then surely I can love others. Oh, but it's not always that easy! "Lord, what if I can't love that one— he'll never change anyway. Or that one—she really is a drag! Oh, and that guy gets on my last nerve! I just don't think I can love like You do!" We can find all kinds of excuses *not* to love people, but we only need one reason to love them. We love them because Christ loved us.

The greatest hindrance to any relationship is the fear of commitment. To protect ourselves in ministry, we often work too hard at creating boundaries. Healthy boundaries are a necessity, but they should be healthy for the people on both sides of the boundaries. I cannot be so protective of myself that I am not willing to get a little dirty or to get truly involved in the lives of the people God has called me to serve. Real ministry is not always pretty and is sometimes downright messy. And sometimes we pay a dear price for loving others in the middle of their mess. They don't always choose the right path, and sometimes the ones we help the most are the ones that hurt us the most. Sometimes I may not think I can go the distance with another. But I have to remember that my commitment to love goes upward and outward: to God first and then to others. Jesus Himself really brings it into perspective. Get a load of how far He really expects us to go! "My command is this: Love each other as I have loved you. Greater love has no one than this: that he **lay down his life** for his friends" (John 15:12-13 NIV emphasis added). He doesn't just expect me to live to love; He expects me to be willing to give up my own life for others. And He didn't ask; He commanded! Loving as Jesus loves requires sacrifice. Staying true to my commitment requires me to continually die to my own self. He challenges me time after time, and through each challenge, I grow stronger in love for others.

I'm personally most comfortable loving those who don't fit in the realms of traditional churches. Sometimes their extreme problems require extreme measures and even more extreme love, at least by traditional standards. I have discovered that I'm actually most comfortable in ministering to the drug addict, the alcoholic, the gang member, or the abused person who is struggling to get out of their circumstances. But I realize that loving to the extreme sometimes requires more from me than I ever thought possible and often far more than I ever desired to give. Extreme love requires extreme patience because I often walk the same path over and over again with the same person. But when I get to the end of my rope, I remember that Jesus loved the same people in His day and time.

Living To Love

"Maggie" (name has been changed) is a cutter. In order to escape intrusive memories or to cope with guilt and shame, she cuts herself. Though most of the outside world has no idea

To Know 'Em Is To Love 'Em

about her secret pain and knows very little about the reality of her past, she has slowly begun to bring her story to light among a few trusted people. It has taken more than forty years for her to speak the truth.

Maggie was raised in a strict "Christian" home, but she was molested by a family member regularly at a very young age and told it was a secret act of love. Unable to tell anyone what was happening, she learned to detach herself mentally and emotionally from the experience of the moment. Dissociation and self-injury became a way of life—a way of escaping reality and pain. It was the only way she could care for herself. As she entered her teen years, the abuse lessened in the number of incidents but dramatically increased in violence. Cutting became a necessary coping mechanism as well as seeking acceptance in other unhealthy relationships. At seventeen, she was violently raped one last time by the abuser. Maggie was emotionless when she soon discovered she was pregnant. Although it went against her convictions, Maggie had no choice but to hide what had happened. She had an abortion—not a clinical abortion since clinics were few and far between in that part of the country in those days. She endured an illegal procedure by a medical student in a home kitchen and then was sent home alone for the abortion to "come to completion." No one knew. She detached—she could shed no tears, grieve no loss, feel no pain, and bear no anger. Maggie had learned to compartmentalize events—to completely separate this event from the rest of her life as if it never happened. The escape prevented her from acknowledging pain so the ordeal didn't visibly affect her job, her education, her ministry, or even her engagement…she thought.

Life went on as usual. Nobody knew her secrets. Maggie carried her guilt and shame into an abusive marriage. Childhood had taught her to keep her secrets well. One by one children were born—each birth adding even more weight to the guilt. She raised her children and served faithfully in ministry for years, but no one would have guessed what went on when no one was looking. The abuse was committed behind closed bedroom doors—even the children were largely unaware. She could easily hide or explain away the cuts and injuries when it became necessary to cope with overwhelming emotions. She buried herself in the lives of others, in overachievement, and busyness. The deepest parts of her guilt and shame belonged in another life, one separate from the life with her family and her ministry. No one could have guessed what went on inside. As her children grew and needed her less and less, her façade began to crumble, and she finally sought help in counseling.

At forty years old, Maggie finally walked away from abuse and her false Christian life and finally found herself at this little church called the Mission. The guilt and shame of her past began to cave in on her, and she withdrew from everyone. She escaped into her old coping mechanisms, cutting her flesh in a desperate attempt to numb the pain she had carried for years. That's where my journey with her began. When she first came to our church, Maggie sat in the very back with her arms folded and her head down. She was unapproachable. No matter how I tried, I couldn't get her to talk to me. She didn't trust anyone. From the first time I met her, I told her there was a reason she was at the Mission—that God had a plan and we would walk with her. She stayed because she didn't have anywhere else to go. That was several years ago. I couldn't have guessed then how long and sometimes how messy and demanding this journey would be.

Her situation is not foreign to me. I have a bachelor of behavioral science degree in psychology and a master's degree in counseling and human development. With my knowledge, it's easy to listen and process her struggle with my mind, but as her friend, I'm learning to listen and understand with my heart. Regardless, I can't "fix" Maggie's broken spirit. I think that is what is most frustrating. As her friend, I can't make her accept grace. She knows Scripture through and through. She comprehends truth and grace with her mind yet struggles to take it from her head to her heart. And I can't be her hero. Only God can. Like the four friends brought the paraplegic before the Lord, all I can do is bring her into His presence.

Walking along with her on this journey, I am learning patience and persistence in friendship. Her stubbornness can be her greatest weakness but also her greatest strength. I see the frailty of the human spirit when she is broken, and I see the strength of Christ in her when she gets back up from a fall. It's sometimes hard to keep up with the twists and turns. In his letter to the Galatians, Paul emphasized the real truth of being a friend like Jesus, "What is important is faith expressing itself in love" (Gal. 5:6 NLT).

As her friend, I'm learning to urge Maggie to voice her shame rather than hiding it in the cutting. But when she won't open up and I can't do anything about it, I'm learning to be quiet and still and know that He is God. And I pray. He hears what she can't speak.

> *In the same way, the Spirit helps us in our weakness. We do not know what we ought to pray for, but the Spirit himself intercedes for us with groans that words cannot express. And he who searches our hearts knows the mind of the Spirit, because the spirit intercedes for the saints in accordance with God's will* (Rom. 8:26-27 NIV).

As her pastor and friend, I wish I had all the answers she needs but I don't. That's not what God requires of me, and it's

The Superman Syndrome

not even what Maggie wants or expects. All I can do is accept her right where she is and in those moments when she can't find hope, I simply love her like Jesus.

STUDY QUESTIONS

1. Name at least three people with whom you are currently ministering through accountability and encouragement in their walk of faith?

_____   _____

_____

2. How are you actively taking time to truly listen and care about the people you encounter on a daily basis?

_____
_____
_____

3. What kind of people do you find most comfortable to love?

_____
_____
_____

4. What kind of people do you find more difficult to love?

_____
_____
_____

Chapter 4

Wanted: Demolition Crew
No Experience Necessary

BEYOND PREJUDICE TO ACCEPTANCE

The way we are with each other is the truest test of our faith. How I treat a brother or sister from day to day, how I react to the sin-scarred wino on the street, how I respond to interruptions from people I dislike, how I deal with normal people in their normal confusion on a normal day may be a better indication of my reverence for life than the anti-abortion sticker on the bumper of my car. We are not pro-life simply because we are warding off death. We are pro-life to the extent that we are men and women for others, all others; to the extent that no human flesh is a stranger to us; to the extent that we can touch the hand of another in love; to the extent that for us there are no 'others'" (Brennan Manning, *The Ragamuffin Gospel*).

In my younger days, I was always an avid sports fan. I would attend all types of sporting events—but not just for the sake of the competition on the playing field. I didn't necessarily care how much either team scored as long as I did! One Saturday morning, a buddy of mine invited me to a Hardin-Simmons University football game with his church. Going to a game with a church group! How much fun could that possibly be? Laughing at the idea, I asked him, "Are there any good-lookin' girls going?"

He was a preacher's kid but a fellow spectator in the games off the field, so he quietly but eagerly assured me so that no one could hear, "Yep!"

"I'm in! What time do we leave?" So later that day, I was sitting on hot metal bleachers at the college stadium, watching the game in the stands much more than the one on the field. After the football game was over, we hurried to the parking lot to beat the traffic, but I hadn't given up on "scoring" just because the football game was over. Out of the corner of my eye, I caught a glimpse of a cute girl as she walked past the stadium gate. I announced my strategy to my buddy, "I'm going to jump the fence and try to catch that girl!"

Knowing my limitations better than I did, he saw flags on the field before I even took off. "Don't do it, Chad! You're gonna get stuck on that fence!"

I was somewhat chunky—okay, a very large kid—and my friend didn't have much confidence in my agility. But the prize was worth the risk, and ignoring his advice, I sprinted—well, I jogged anyway—to the fence and began to climb. With ease, I launched my body to the top of the fence, but as I began to push myself off to the other side, wouldn't you know it—my pants got caught on the fence. My so-called friend found great humor in my hopeless predicament as I yelled at him, "Man, quit laughing and help me!"

Seconds ticked by but it seemed like forever. He just stood there laughing at the show as I pleaded, "Help me, man! This really isn't funny!" But he was evidently convinced that it was hilarious.

Looking back at this humiliation now, I understand what Malcolm X meant when he said, "Nobody can give you freedom. Nobody can give you equality or justice or anything. If you're a man, you take it."

I had no choice but to free myself by pushing off the fence with everything I had. R-r-r-i-i-p-p-p! I fell to the ground. As I picked myself up from the dirt, I glanced across the street and saw a family laughing hysterically and pointing in my direction. With a sickening sixth sense, I slowly raised my eyes to the top of the fence and confirmed my worst fear. Well, there was a flag on this play—a bright white one! Dangling on the top of the fence for all to see was half of my tighty whities! And there I stood exposed while thousands of people (I'm sure it was!) passed by on their way out of the stadium. I could almost swear the majority of them were cute girls just like the one I had been chasing. Needless to say, I caught their attention! My strategy succeeded!

If only I had taken just a minute to consider my buddy's warning, I might have spared myself this embarrassment. But in spite of the indignity I had suffered, I still accomplished something important that day. I saw an opportunity to kindle a relationship and I went after it. I didn't let a chain-link wall separate me from someone I wanted to know—even though she and so many others got to know me far more than I anticipated.

The Superman Syndrome

BUILD 'EM UP AND KNOCK 'EM DOWN!

Throughout the world, walls are built to divide one space from another—providing protection from dangerous elements, one yard from another, public property from private, neighborhood from neighborhood, or one country from another. The great poet Robert Frost penned, "Good fences make good neighbors." On some days I totally agree with him, like when the neighbor's maniac dog won't shut up. The fence helps me remain a "good" neighbor. Without it, I would cross that boundary and shoot that annoying dog! So the interesting thing about fences is that they have the potential to become beneficial or detrimental in purpose.

On November 9, 1989 I sat in class at school and witnessed history in the making as television air waves proclaimed the news that the Berlin Wall was coming down. The news anchor declared, "For twenty-eight long years, the wall divided East and West Berlin…" The barrier was built to separate democratic West Germany from Communist-occupied East Germany. East Germans didn't want their people to get out or the Westerners to get in, and they meant serious business. Official accounts report that over 171 people were killed trying to escape from the East to the West between 1961 and 1989, although prominent victims' groups declare that at least 261 people were killed while trying to flee. The world celebrated when the wall that was built to brutally divide people was finally destroyed and the Cold War ended.

If we were completely honest, every person that ever walked the earth except Jesus has constructed walls of prejudice. We build a barricade to keep out people we fear or don't understand—anyone who is different—just like the Communist government constructed the Berlin wall to separate itself from the Western world and ideology. In American society, we cry out for

Wanted: Demolition Crew

tolerance, but on both sides of any issue, intolerance abounds. Let's peel off the top layer and look inside for a few minutes. Prejudice is simply preconceived judgment against an entire group based on prior experience with only a part of them. Our prejudice against people or ideas is born from our personal or traditional experience. Our experience ultimately determines how we view others. Prejudice is even passed down from generation to generation based on experiences of ancestors we never even met. We hate simply because those before us hated. How often we cling to heritage and hateful traditions over long forgotten or misinterpreted injustices! It's the Hatfields and McCoys again and again. We allow past experience as we perceive it to supersede knowledge of a present truth, and we despise people unjustly.

On September 11, 2001, the United States was viciously attacked in a series of suicide missions by Islamic terrorists. As I watched image after horrifying image on camera, I witnessed something incredibly beautiful. Yes—beautiful. Now before you slam this book shut and label me as pro-terrorist, hear me out! With overwhelming sorrowful emotion and tears running down my cheeks, I witnessed unfathomable pain and terror as the towers fell. The indelible images of people jumping from buildings are etched in my memory forever as news stations broadcasted the video again and again. Yet in the midst of all this terrible evil and pain, I saw real beauty as the living dug through heaps of ashes and rubble with all the human strength they could muster to rescue those who were buried. Black and white, Muslim and Christian, Catholic and agnostic, rich and poor, young and old—every social boundary in everyday life was crossed as people from all walks of life linked together to rescue every surviving soul. On September 11th, prejudice disappeared in New York City in the minutes after the towers fell and was instantly replaced with an amazing outpouring of love and grace as people set aside their individual experience to share a common goal for the good of all. We witnessed true beauty rising from ashes of hatred and vengeance as people began to accept each other in this time of need in spite of race, religion, culture, or creed.

A Neighborhood Tale

Only after suffering unimaginable tragedy did New Yorkers finally knock down their walls of prejudice to reach out to their next-door neighbors. How many of us are just the same? Many of us, churched and unchurched alike, could quote Jesus' greatest commandments, but the significance of His teaching doesn't impact us until disaster strikes. In Luke 10, we read the historical account that challenged religious and moral thinking of the day and has influenced today's world in or out of Christian circles.

A young well-educated lawyer asked Jesus a fundamental question, "Teacher, how do I get to heaven?"

Jesus pointed to the law of Moses but to be sure the lawyer understood, He asked the man to recite it. The lawyer recalled the ancient words without effort, "Love the Lord your God with all your heart and with all your soul and with all your strength and with all your mind. And love your neighbor as yourself."

"OK, then do it," Jesus replied.

Saying the words out loud made obedience to the law seem a little more costly than the young lawyer had bargained for. In Christ's presence, the full meaning of the words hit home and dear old Prejudice reared his ugly head. The ambitious lawyer hoped Jesus would make it easier on him, "Well, then who's my neighbor?"

Haven't we all stood in this brash young man's shoes? But Jesus leaves no room for excuses, and He made his point so very

Wanted: Demolition Crew

clear through His telling of one of the most widely-known stories in literature.

A Jewish countryman was traveling on a lonely road when he was hijacked by a band of thieves. He was stripped, beaten, robbed, and left for dead. A priest came upon the helpless victim. But he was a leader of the church and couldn't be bothered with this pettiness. He had much to do and wasn't about to soil his own holy robes with the likes of this man. The priest carried a wall of prejudice around him constructed of his own self-importance and piety. In pure and simple words, he was a snob. The business he was about rated much higher on the scale than a fallen man who was half-dead anyway. The priest moved to the other side of the road to avoid the mess and hurried on his way without a backward glance.

Then along came a Levite, a temple assistant more or less, and one who knew and understood church law. He was curious enough to walk over and take a look at the wounded man lying in the road. Maybe he even nudged the poor guy to see if he was still alive and wondered what a shame this had happened. But in the end, the Levite didn't actually know the dude, so his pitiful condition was really none of his concern. Up went his wall of prejudice built with stones of apathy and indifference. To do anything would be too much bother, and it was his day off. So he went on his merry way.

Finally, a foreigner—a Samaritan—came upon the injured man. Jews considered people of his kind as mixed breeds and impure. Most Jews would rather spit on a Samaritan than speak to him, much less touch one. This guy had every right to build a wall made of generational hatred and tradition. Let's get real—who would blame him if just passed on by? He had absolutely no reason to play Dudley Do-Right here! But the Samaritan set aside their differences and looked on the man with compassion.

He patched up his wounds the best he could, gently loaded him on his own donkey, and took him to a motel in town where he cared for him through the night. The next morning, he paid the desk clerk in advance so that the injured man could stay there for several days while he recuperated. He even paid extra so that the staff would care for him and then promised to reimburse any more expenses for the patient when he returned on his way home. Wow! Talk about going above and beyond the call of duty! As far as anyone knows, the Samaritan didn't even know this stranger's name.

When Jesus finished the story, He asked the young lawyer which one of the travelers was the best neighbor. Well, duh! Any of us could answer that easily, right? The Samaritan, of course. But the guy's prejudice was so strong, he couldn't even say that nasty word. He could only say that it was the one who showed mercy to the robbed man. Jesus commanded the young lawyer and He commands us to do the same, "Then be a Good Samaritan."

Oh, but it's sometimes so much easier said than done! Most of us relate more closely to the young lawyer than we like to admit. Can you imagine? Jesus told him to be exactly who the Jews hated, a Samaritan! Of course, Jesus didn't define people by their heritage. He defined them by love. We might even see glimpses of ourselves in the priest and Levite—too good, too busy, and too indifferent. We'd like to boast that we are just like the good Samaritan, but in truth, we get a little uncomfortable when we realize that our "neighbor" is anyone in our range of contact—whether we like that person or not!

My Own Samaritan Experience

The apostle Paul urges us:

Wanted: Demolition Crew

Be completely humble and gentle; be patient, bearing with one another in love. Make every effort to keep the unity of the Spirit through the bond of peace. There is one body and one Spirit—just as you were called to one hope when you were called—one Lord, one faith, one baptism; one God and Father of ALL, who is over ALL and through ALL and in ALL (Eph. 4:2-6 NIV, emphasis added).

God is the Father of all, but each one of us are individually responsible to love each other. One by one, He calls us to break down walls that divide us and build unity in their place. "Chad, I want you to love your neighbor…"

As I rounded the final corner on my way home from church one day, I noticed an elderly black man walking down the street, trying to juggle four plastic bags of groceries at the same time while beads of sweat streamed down his face in the hot afternoon sun. God whispered in a voice I know all too well, "Chad, pick up that poor old man. Look at him! He can hardly walk carrying all those heavy groceries! Chad, love your neighbor…"

When He calls you by name, you gotta listen! But I didn't know the old man from Adam, and he certainly didn't know me. We didn't have anything in common at all. I tried to talk myself and God out of this crazy idea. But God prodded my spirit, "Chad, where is your faith?"

Uh oh, He said my name again! No more hesitation. I pulled into a nearby driveway. With a trembling voice and still wondering what we could possibly talk about, I offered the weary old black man a ride. His eyes lit up and smiling, he said, "Son, I sho' would 'preciate it!"

Sticky with sweat, he achingly climbed in my passenger seat. "You know what, son? Let me tell you somethin'. My entire life, I always heard black folks talkin' so bad about white folks that I basically started to become prejudiced myself. Today, I was in the store buyin' my groceries and was short fourteen cents. The clerk—a black man—told me I'd have to put somethin' back. I go to that store every day, and he knows I would've paid him back! That stubborn clerk wouldn't give me fourteen cents! All of a sudden, a white man behind me handed the clerk a five-dollar bill to pay my debt, and he even gave me the change! Then as I was walkin' back carryin' these heavy groceries you—a white teenage boy—gives me, an old black man, a ride home. I'm sick o' hearin' 'bout prejudice! Everyone bleeds red; everyone is the same."

In my own prejudice, I hadn't considered he might struggle with the same in reverse. "You know what, sir? It's not about blacks, whites, Hispanics, and so forth. It's about God's children—we are *all* God's children."

"Why did you pick me up? Look at me. I'm a total stranger," he asked as he looked at me.

With a little laugh, I jokingly admitted, "Well, me and Jesus got in a wrestling match and He won! In all honesty, I love Jesus and I love all people."

As I drove him home, I calculated how far he would have walked carrying his heavy load two and a half miles under a burning sun! When he got out of my truck he shook my hand, saying, "Son, thank ya for showin' me that in this world, people are all the same and that there are still good people out there that love all people. But most of all, there are people who show their love for Jesus by their actions. One more thing…No matter what others say or do that might cause ya to stumble or hurt you, always keep the faith that you have showed me today. You have truly blessed my life!"

As I left him, I was glad God had urged me to pick up the old man. With certainty, I knew that elderly black gentleman helped me far more that day than I helped him, and I thanked God for my Samaritan experience.

I shared the incident with my church the following Sunday. After the service, a middle-aged white woman rushed up to tell me the rest of the story. "Pastor Chad, I have to tell you something! Three days after you picked up that elderly black man, I picked up that very same man on North 10th Street!"

I said, "You're kidding! How do you know it was him?"

She went on, "When I picked him up, he just shook his head as he got in the car. Thinking his car must have broken down, I asked him what was wrong. He said that nothing was wrong. He was just overwhelmed at the fact that I was the second white person to pick him up this week. Then he told me the story of a young man who picked him up a few days earlier. He said that boy shared his faith with him! That's so awesome! It was you, Pastor Chad!"

Years have come and gone since I met that old gentleman, and I often wonder about him as I drive home on hot summer days...if he is well or even still alive. No doubt though, I will see him again one day in eternity.

Because God called me to offer one small act of kindness, self-imposed walls of prejudice came tumbling down, and the event impacted me, a weary black gentleman, and an entire congregation.

UNITED WE STAND, DIVIDED WE FALL

As I live and breathe each day, I'm finally beginning to fathom why Jesus stressed the necessity of loving our neighbor at any cost. In a world plagued with hatred, dishonesty, and hopelessness, the one element needed to release the waters of change so they trickle over dams of prejudice is that followers of Jesus Christ obediently extend His love and mercy across every private barrier regardless of experience or tradition. Jesus reached beyond every social and cultural bias—color, economic status, age, dialect, gender, and caste—and centered on redemption for each and every one of us. John 3:16 says that God so loved the world, the *whole* world, so much that He gave His one and only Son to die in our stead.

Prejudice of any kind is a wall that obstructs our view. Because we build our walls so high and wide, we cannot see anything beyond them. We assume that sights we have never even beheld are without merit or beauty. With all of my heart, I believe that each one of us is uniquely created in the image of our Creator and beauty is found in our diversity, but God never intended that our differences should divide us. If we dared to accept our differences in light of our Creator, we would witness the amazing dawn of a brand new horizon. We would finally see each other and love each other in the same way that New York citizens finally perceived one another on that fateful day in the heart-wrenching aftermath of the 9/11 catastrophe. Isn't it ludicrous and bizarre? In reality, we often hate entire sects of the human race that have committed no crime against us. Individual men may commit crimes against us but not entire races or kinds of people. A whole race or nation isn't responsible for one man's actions.

Our differences in culture or appearance don't have the power to pursue good or evil. Good and evil intent comes from the heart not from our outer appearance. We think others less than we are "just because"—their skin may be different, their size, their gender, their wealth, their church, their customs, or simply their language. Any reason seems justified if it proclaims someone isn't like us. One's differences as we perceive them warrant another human being as "not good enough" and undeserving of love. Even the Nazis thought that true perfection was accomplished by genetics—blonde hair, blue eyes, and fair skin. We make up all sorts of excuses, but in truth we are often blind to the atrocity and injustice of our own hatred.

When we let the walls crumble and fall away, and view the broad expanse of life as it really is without obstruction, we realize that our prejudices exist although no crime has ever actually been committed against us and no evil intended toward us. Our blindness and shortsightedness are actually caused by dirty spots on our own focal lenses. If we even dare to remove the spots that limit our sight and venture beyond our own imagined perception, we might view mankind in fullness with its vast array of unique diversities. Suddenly, we may behold the rich horizon of human life with awe just as we would relish and cherish the many hues blended together in a beautiful sunrise. Rather than allowing our past traditions and experiences to divide us, we should blend them with the love and mercy of Jesus Christ to unite us. The walls of prejudice and intolerance would crumble in the dawn of a whole new Son-rise.

> *For everything that was written in the past was written to teach us so that through endurance and the encouragement of the Scriptures, we might have hope. May the God who gives endurance and encouragement give you a spirit of unity among yourselves as you follow Christ Jesus so that with one heart and mouth, you may glorify the God and Father of our Lord Jesus Christ* (Rom. 15:4-6 NIV).

I pray that as we persistently live out our faith as followers of Christ, we will continue to witness or even be a laborer on the working crew in the demolition of more and more Berlin walls.

STUDY QUESTIONS

1. Be completely honest and objective regarding your own prejudices. What walls of prejudice have you constructed over the years, and how have they affected your life and ministry?

___

2. As you walk in the footsteps of Jesus, how are you crossing every social and cultural bias—color, economic status, age, dialect, and gender to reach the lost?

___

3. Have you recently displayed any small acts of kindness that has helped your self-imposed walls of prejudice come tumbling down?

___

4. Describe a time in your life when you have been impacted by a "Samaritan experience."

___

Chapter 5

Losin' Our Religion!

BEYOND CHURCH TO EVERYWHERE YOU ARE

I used to be an avid golfer. If I could get away with any excuse on a cool, breezy afternoon, I'd be out on the golf course soaking it all up. There's nothing like it. On one such day in my single years, I was taking full advantage of the beautiful Texas sunshine and getting in eighteen holes. The problem is the fact that I do live in Texas and that hot Texas sunshine blazed into my afternoon while the cool early breezes evaporated into nothing but hot air. Now a real golfer doesn't abandon his game just because of a little heat, so I wasn't about to give up my game. I was soon drenched with sweat. Just as I finished the last hole, blaming my poor score on the heat, my cell phone rang. My girlfriend was just reminding me that I had promised earlier in the week to meet her at the movies that evening. Golf wasn't the only game I played in those days before Christ, so I chivalrously pretended I hadn't forgotten our date and told her that I'd be there. I looked at my watch then and the heat was really on! I didn't realize I had enjoyed my golf game quite so long, and the movie started in fifteen minutes! I figured that I had just enough time to get across town to the theatre without her knowing I'd put our date on the back burner for my golf game.

I made it to the theatre just as the previews were beginning to roll. My girlfriend had already gone inside. I quickly found her sitting four rows from the top on the left side. I slipped in beside her and got comfortable, stretching my arms on the backs of the chairs on each side of me—classic Romeo move. She'd soon forget any frustration that I was running just a little behind. But my move went sour because in a split second, I got a whiff of my afternoon golf game, and it was obvious I needed a shower! I nonchalantly excused myself and went to the restroom and got the answer to my unasked prayer. Right there in the bathroom, bold and beautiful, was a vending machine filled with various generic colognes. This theatre must have been a real Romeo hangout! I didn't care—this machine could save my date all for the price of one dollar! I purchased a packet of cologne and doused myself with it. Ahh! Much better...I thought. I climbed the dimly lit stairs back to my seat and once again assumed my relaxed position with my arm stretched over my girlfriend's chair.

Quicker than a starving dog can latch on to a bone, my girlfriend choked up in revulsion, "Oh, my gosh! What is that smell?" Evidently my quick dollar solution didn't mix well with my golf game aroma. I had done my best to mask my sweat smell, but cheap cologne didn't eliminate it. Instead, it intensified the stench!

It's a sad reality and harsh truth that my girlfriend's disgusted response to my body odor was not so different than many people's response to the modern-day church. We have the gospel of Christ at our fingertips—our most powerful resource to draw the lost nearer to Him. But so many of us have been caught up in the game and been in the "sun" far too long. And let's face it, sometimes our "religion" stinks! Paul inspired the church at Ephesus with these words:

> *Be imitators of God, therefore, as dearly loved children and live a life of love, just as Christ loved us and gave himself up for us as a fragrant offering and sacrifice to God* (Eph. 5:1-2 NIV).

It's that simple: *live a life of love*—the same love that Christ showed on the Cross for you and for me. And we must live His love in our homes, in our communities, and most definitely in our churches. But somehow we've turned His simple gospel of love into a hot windy manuscript of do's and don'ts, and rules and regulations. We try to dress it up with vain attempts at different techniques, worship styles, and the latest, greatest church fads. Like cheap cologne, these efforts don't get rid of the stench—we're just masking the smell with religious facades and happy faces. We put on a good front, and we look good from a distance; but as the lost and the unchurched draw nearer to us in hopes of finding what is missing in their lives, the stench becomes even more foul. Too often the church reeks of religiosity, arrogance, and hypocrisy, and all the attractive formulas and sweet-smelling coffeebars can't begin to cover it up! And the lost souls outside the church aren't the only ones who suffer.

BURNING QUESTIONS

Many of you may sputter in contempt at these words. I understand completely—they aren't easy to read and even harder to take to heart when we look objectively at ourselves and our own churches from the viewpoint of an outsider rather than from our position of a member. Are we, individually or as the body of Christ, a sweet fragrant offering of love to God? Like it or not, the church repulses many people, because from where they are sitting, Christianity is a religion driven by rules, regulations, and condemnation. Those of us on the inside think far too much of ourselves, and that's who we show the world rather than the Christ we profess. Those on the outside hear the "saved" professing a message of love in one breath and spewing hatred, judgment, and holier-than-thou attitudes toward the "unsaved" in the next. All too often in our efforts to draw the lost into the church, our religious hypocrisy drives them out. They don't know that sometimes the "faith" we show isn't the Jesus we should be.

"Turn or burn, you workers of iniquity! You will burn in the lake of fire!... Repent or burn in hell!" Street preachers yell and scream fire and brimstone on every corner in the crowded and bawdy streets of New Orleans during Mardi Gras. I've seen and heard it all personally when I've had the opportunity to reach out to the revelers of Mardi Gras in my ministry. And I mean I've seen everything in that city! For the sake of calling this a Christian book, I'll spare you the details of the obscene acts, lewd behavior, and lawlessness I've witnessed in those streets. It is undeniably true that sin runs rampant, and there is a need for the gospel there. As heartbreaking as it is to see those people live out so many sins they will later regret, it is even more heartbreaking to witness the even more tragic and recurring picture of street preachers holding up annoying and deafening air horns while shrieking hell and damnation at the Mardi Gras merrymakers, rather than sharing the love of Christ with them.

Our team's mission one year was simply to pass out food, sleeping bags, and hygiene kits to the gutter punks and teen runaways. We weren't yelling or screaming or shaking our fingers in their faces. We just handed out the needed items and shared the gospel when given an opportunity. Night after night, we observed the same pattern that pierces my heart to this day. One after another, these gutter punks would ask us the same questions. One kid, probably about sixteen years old, sauntered up to me, "Hey, mister! Let me ask you a question…"

"Sure, man. Fire away!" I said.

"Why aren't you like that fat man on the corner screaming at all of us that we're going to hell?"

I looked at him with a complete sense of sadness and replied hesitantly, "Well, the truth is that if we don't know Jesus, we will go to hell. But I just don't believe in his approach, bro. I approach people with love."

That gutter punk seemed much less of a punk than the street preachers in the next moment because his words would stick with me the rest of my life, "I would definitely follow Christ if there were more people like you that followed Him."

As Christians, how did we miss the mark? How do we hate and judge when we are called to love and inspire? So many Christians just don't get it: we're not here to preach death but to share life. It does smell pretty rank, doesn't it? Jesus didn't need cheap cologne—He made a promise to the disciples:

> *Do not let your hearts be troubled. Trust in God; trust also in me. In my Father's house are many rooms; if it were not so, I would have told you. I am going there to prepare a place for you. And if I go and prepare a place for you, I will come back and take you to be with me that you also may be where I am…I am the way, the truth, and the life… Anyone who has seen me has seen the Father* (John 14:1-3, 6, 9 NIV).

Jesus rarely spoke of death without regard to life. His primary message was His love and the promise of eternal life not eternal doom. Through Him, the disciples saw the Father. Through us, the unsaved see Jesus Christ. My conversation continued with the wayward teen, "Bro, don't base your faith in Jesus Christ on people that scream hate. Base it on the true foundation of the gospel: Jesus' love for you!"

In a matter of minutes another gutter punk approached me, "Man, I need you to answer a question for me."

With a little anxiety, I answered "Sure."

I was beginning to expect the question I knew was coming, "Why aren't you like those people?"

"What people?"

"Those people over there holding up a sign that says, 'Turn or burn,'" he said, pointing.

"Why do you ask? Do you like those guys?"

Without hesitation, he answered "No way!"

I informed him that I didn't really like them either—at least not their tactics. He was surprised at my admission. "What? You don't like them either? Why not? They're Christians."

Once again, I was able to explain that those guys weren't representing the God I worship and follow. I was able to share that my God is a loving God who cherishes and loves every human being no matter what they've done. Please don't misunderstand me—I wholeheartedly recognize the fact that Christ will return and bring judgment. I am not condoning sin of any kind, nor am I minimizing the consequences of sin. Those who have rejected Christ will not receive the promise of heaven. The unsaved will suffer in hell, but I believe with all that I am that Christ will passionately pursue all of humanity *with love* until rapture's alarm clock rings. Scare tactics like those demonstrated along Bourbon Street give the unsaved a tainted perspective of who God is. The very people for whom God loved so much that He gave His own Son as a sacrifice—they want nothing of this hateful and vengeful God who is eager to damn people to hell as preached and screeched in the streets. Hellfire ministry gives the impression that all Christians are walking judges, instead of walking commercials of hope and love. But that isn't how Christ taught us to minister. Others know Him by our actions and our words. Jesus always spoke love rather than condemnation, "By this all men will know that you are my disciples, if you love one another" (John 13:35 NIV).

The church itself didn't "just happen." They had to work at it, keep working at it, and grow in unity and in love. Paul's letters were to the churches, teaching them how God has called each one to be the Body of Christ—but it was never about condemnation, always loving people with the gospel:

Their responsibility [speaking of the church] *is to equip God's people to do His work and build up* [notice it says, build up, not tear down] *the church, the body of Christ. This will continue until we all come to such unity in our faith and knowledge of God's Son that we will be mature in the Lord, measuring up to the full and complete standard of Christ. Then we will no longer be immature like children. We won't be tossed and blown about by every wind of new teaching. We will not be influenced when people try to trick us with lies so clever they sound like the truth. Instead,* **we will speak the truth in love***, growing in every way more and more like Christ, who is the head of his body, the church. He makes the whole body fit together perfectly. As each part does its own special work, it helps the other parts grow, so that the whole body is healthy and growing and FULL OF LOVE!* (Eph. 4:12-16 NLT, emphasis added)

COMPARATIVELY SPEAKING...

It's true that there are probably many more loving Christians than hateful ones, but it is also a hard reality that most people see the worst long before they see the best—most likely because the hateful ones yell the loudest and get the most camera coverage. But because of the few, the very opposite of what we are supposed to be is at the forefront of all that the lost community sees. So I have to ask myself, because any true change, no matter what it is, begins with me, "Do people see Jesus in me? I may be the only Christ they see—the only Christ they know. Would they want to love me back?" Remember Paul's words because that is how we should present the gospel to all people: *we will speak the truth in love.*

Most of us would readily deny that we aren't like those street preachers spewing condemnation. Jesus said, "Anyone who has seen me has seen the Father..." And we are to be like Him. So when people look at me, do they see Him? What about you? Do they feel His love or His condemnation? Struggle through this with me for just a moment. What if we just lose our "religion"? Would the true gospel of love be defined by the way we as Christians live our lives? Maybe—just maybe—if we would pursue our Maker with all that we are rather than statistics and church numbers, we would be living and joyful evidence of the Christ within. Maybe people would see something different about us and the stagnant odor of hypocrisy and complacency would be replaced with the sweet aroma of Christ. Sadly enough, Joe Aldrich, the former president of Multnomah Bible College, truthfully stated:

> The best argument for Christianity is Christians: their joy, their certainty, their completeness. But the strongest argument against Christianity is also Christians—when

they are somber and joyless, when they are self-righteous and smug in complacent consecration, when they are narrow and repressive, then Christianity dies a thousand deaths (Joe Aldrich, *Lifestyle Evangelism: Learning to Open Your Life to Those Around You*).

Religious hypocrites have been around for centuries. In fact, Jesus' strongest words were spoken not to the unsaved or the sinner but rather to the sanctimonious—the religious leaders. He often chastised them and used them as the example of what Christians shouldn't be. He abhorred self-righteousness and spoke against that sin more than any other. He even told a parable in Luke 18 to those who struggled with pride, comparing the self-righteous with the humble hearted.

Two men went into the temple to pray—one a Pharisee and the other a tax collector. Pharisees lived their whole lives in front of others—making sure all others saw their deeds and sacrifice. This one was no different. He stood up in the center of the temple and prayed loudly, more for all the people in earshot to take notice of his "holiness," rather than for God to hear. He made a dramatic production of his oratory prayer, "Oh, dear God, thank You that I am not a sinner like all these others—thieves, crooks, adulterers—and especially not like this tax collector over here! I fast twice a week and I pay my tithe faithfully. You have nothing on me—I'm good! Amen."

In those days, tax collectors were hated and despised because they were known for their thievery and unscrupulous practices. This tax collector knew his sin and imperfections. He stood at a distance from the temple altar in complete humility, unworthy to come before the throne of the Most High God. He couldn't even look up to the heavens in his prayers. Instead, he bowed his head low in shame and beat his chest, "God, have mercy on me, a sinner."

Both men came to pray all right, but they came into the presence of the Lord with completely different attitudes! The Pharisee thought God was Burger King, and he approached God's drive-through window eager to get his order his way, as if God greeted His customers, "Welcome to My presence where you can always 'have it your way—have it your way.' May I take your order?" Notice the self-centered prayer: I…I…I." Was God's glory first and foremost in his heart or his own glory? Can't you just see him—this fat Pharisee eloquently proclaiming his good works in his prayer. He had to tell God how good he was because it didn't truly show in his actions, but anyone who heard must have thought, "Wow! What a spiritual and holy man he is!"

The Pharisee relied solely on his own authority and good works before God, but the pendulum swings to the farthest opposite direction when the tax collector prayed. He knew he was nothing without God. Stumbling over his words and shaking in fear and brokenness, he brought his confession before the Lord. He relied not on his own measure but on divine grace and compassion to set him right with God. He was a sinner in desperate need of redemption. His prayer was the one that brought joy to his Maker's heart. If anyone else had even heard his prayer or saw his tears, they must have thought, "Wow! I wonder what he did wrong!"

Jesus made it clear that the tax collector in his humility, not the Pharisee, was the one who went home justified before God. He cautions all of us about self-righteousness,

If you walk around with your nose in the air, you're going to end up flat on your face, but if you're content to be simply yourself, you will become more than yourself (Luke 18:14 MSG).

Losin' Our Religion

With a broken heart, I recognize that there are times when I can find myself in both of these men's shoes. Sometimes I am so broken before God, I can hardly find the words to ask for God's indescribable grace to cover me once again. Yet all too often, I find myself with my chest puffed out like the Pharisee, proclaiming to God all that I have done for Him. I may not be like those Mardi Gras street preachers, but a loathsome realization settles deep inside when I realize that sometimes in my arrogance, people see me more than they see my Jesus. We've all done it, seen it, and tallied up our salvation score card. As Christian leaders, we are quick to chalk up how many people we have "led to the Lord," but we never seem to count how many we have driven away from Christ's saving grace through our random acts of gossip, judgment, self-righteousness, and lack of compassion, mercy, and integrity. We may not be spewing "Turn or Burn" slogans through bullhorns or pointing fingers at those who are worse sinners than we are, but are we really any better? Arrogance is still arrogance in any form; and too often we, the church, are a poor representation of the One who defines real love.

THE BUCK STOPS HERE!

How do we make sure that we don't give God a bad rep? Leave it to humans to ruin a perfectly good thing when we try to dress ourselves up on the fast track so we look better than the rest. We're like the potato, a vegetable that in its simplest cooked form—baked—is incredibly loaded with nutrients—potassium, iron, vitamins B and C, and others. But baking takes time, doesn't it? In our fast food mentality, we want everything now—right now. So what do we do? We take a nutritious potato, slice it up, and chunk it in gallons of hot oil and rob it of all its nutrients while adding fat and cholesterol just because we want French fries! Isn't it ironic how we defile simplicity and purity? Like the French fries, we take the simple and pure gospel of love and mercy and shove it in a religious vat of hot grease. We rob His message of all its goodness in our own self-righteousness…just like the fat Pharisee. When I first stumbled across Mahatma Gandhi's well-known words, tears fell down my face at the shameful truth of them, "If it weren't for Christians, I'd be a Christian."

Sounds like the church needs to get it together, doesn't it? So what do we do about it? Well, the buck stops here! Right at the church door! But we *are* the church—it isn't a building, a denomination, or a social club. So your door—your office, your classroom, your home—is the church door, as is mine. The buck stops right where you and I stand.

So if the buck stops with us, what do we, the pastors and church leaders, do with it? Of course the responsibility lies with anyone who calls themselves Christian, but as leaders we should be the first to exemplify Christ. We can't blame the world on this one. The lost world can't be blamed for what it doesn't know. And we can't blame all the other churches because we are the church. We must accept the fact that too many of us—perhaps all of us at times—have turned the gospel of Christ into something it isn't.

We don't get to pick and choose who becomes part of the Body with us. Our job is to show His love to them, and He will do the rest. It's that simple. There's no need to clutter it up. I can start right where I am, and you can start right where you are. Together, we can both make a difference even if it's one new Christian at a time. In my conversations with the two young teens at Mardis Gras who expressed a desire for a gospel of love and grace, my view of the church began to change. I first had to take a look inside my own heart and my own church.

I realized that the church in Christ's day wasn't so different from today's church—it just used different tactics and different words. I can compare the street preachers to the biblical Pharisees in so many ways. Even the first Christian churches had their issues with arrogance and self-righteousness. It's not a new problem and no small wonder why Jesus had so much to say about it.

Did you know that some Jewish males in the first Christian churches prayed like the holier-than-thou Pharisee in Jesus' parable, thanking God that they weren't a Gentile, a slave, or a woman? But God spoke through Paul against ANY form of judgment, condemnation, and division. We've all got what it takes to be heirs of the kingdom.

You are all sons of God through faith in Christ Jesus, for all of you who were baptized into Christ have clothed yourselves with Christ. There is neither Jew nor Greek, slave nor free, male nor female, for you are all one in Christ Jesus (Gal. 3:26-28 NIV).

Did you get that? If we call ourselves Christian, we should all be clothed with Christ to look like Him! No condemnation, no division, just His love. In the midst of my awakening, I realized that the church should be a sanctuary for everyone who needs a safe haven, not a prison for the worst of us or a country club for the most elite.

The church has painted a poor picture of Christ for far too long, and we need to get back to the simplicity of His pure message: LOVE. And with love comes grace. We each must accept responsibility. Change begins with each one of us. We help each other and we love each other at all costs. The first thing we do is to lay down all judgment. It's not my job to force the street preachers to abandon their hell and damnation tactics, but I could make a greater effort to be the church even to them—to share a gospel of love and grace to the gutter punks and to the street preachers alike. The street preachers undoubtedly want the same thing that I want—that others might be redeemed through Jesus Christ. Their passion for it just took a turn. How quickly and easily we lose our compassion and become pretentious and self-righteous when we dwell on others' wrongs and our rights. We may be saved and sanctified, but we have no right to look down our noses at anyone.

Regardless of who screams contempt at us or who "looks" holier or more attractive on the outside, we must stand up for the true gospel of Christ. We must do our part. We are His hands and His feet and His voice reaching out to those who haven't heard the message of His love and mercy. We must be determined to become the Body of Christ by His design, not our own:

He makes the whole Body fit together perfectly. As each part does its own special work, it helps the other parts grow, so that the whole body is healthy and growing and full of love (Eph. 4:16 NLT).

Barstool Theology

So how does that Body fit together? What might it look like? During my younger years, it was not uncommon to find me chillin' on a stool in one of the local bars with a drink in hand. Though many would say that I flushed away my youth in a haze of alcohol and hangovers, those years actually cultivated a vision for my life, my ministry, and my church though it would take a few years to figure that out. Keep in mind that a little manure fertilizes and produces the most abundant crops so what is waste to one person is pure possibility to another. God doesn't waste a single opportunity to make good out of our worst. In light of that, one night with a little bit of liquor—okay, a lot of liquor—in my system, I remember asking myself, "Why do people go to the bars?" Of course this type of a question is usually rhetorical and only asked by dedicated teetotalers. But sometimes after ingesting a substantial amount of alcohol, I sought out the deeper questions and the meaning of life. "Why do people go to bars?" What a question! I have no defense for the wanderings of my inebriated mind and maybe the answer wouldn't shake the world on its axis, but my rhetorical sarcasm gradually became a real and illuminating pursuit of truth even after I sobered up.

Now before you commit me to an asylum or throw your hands up and call me a hopeless heretic, hear me out. The church can learn a thing or two from the local bar. Sometimes we the church think that we have life and ministry all figured out, but as long as there are still lost and lonely people in the community outside of the church, we still have a lot to learn about reaching them. As the Body of Christ, we should turn our focus to the needs of those who swear to never enter our doors. In order to do that, we need to meet people right where they are and take a good hard look at what draws them into relationships with others.

So let's take the perspective of one sitting on the corner barstool in a local tavern. Why do people go to bars? A few of the most obvious reasons are to drink, to listen to music, to socialize with friends, and to dance. Now let's dig a little deeper. What causes a person to be a regular at a particular bar? For one thing it's probably the local "hot spot" where your friends or people just like you hang out. The music is good, the atmosphere is relaxed, and you don't have to dress up to feel welcomed. You can be yourself. Remember Norm from the T.V.

show *Cheers*? He had his own special stool which everybody knew to save for him, where he sat every night drinking beer. He's a regular, commonsense kind of guy everybody loves.

What can the church possibly learn from a bar? I looked at this question from Norm's perspective. When I did, I came up with the three following important lessons.

Barstool Lesson Number One: Create an atmosphere that welcomes and relaxes the average stranger. This is only the beginning as we break down the barriers that keep the lost outside the church doors. The church should not just be accessible to those who have the proper clothes or the proper "Christian" look. The church community must invite all people to come just as they are. People shouldn't have to fluff up, puff up, or make up just to get inside. We should welcome people just as they are, without any façades and pretenses.

No matter where you come from, what race you are, how much or how little money is in your pocket, whether you live in a box or a house—it's all useless information in the friendly neighborhood bar. My own church has made this our mission. We strive to be "a church open to all people." Regardless of fame, wealth, or status quo, each individual needs to know he or she is accepted and loved. Even Paul has challenged the church to "Accept one another, then, just as Christ accepted you…" (Rom. 15:7 NIV).

The gospel of Christ is for all people, but the individual churches have developed this mindset that they can handpick their members. As the Body of Christ, we must make a greater effort to truly accept others as Christ accepts them and love as He loves. We have to learn to take people for who they are and what they are right this minute and offer hope. God will do the rest.

Losin' Our Religion

Barstool Lesson Number Two: The church members must purposefully get to know each other and every person that walks through the doors. One of the biggest myths about bars is that customers go there every night to meet new people. They may not know anyone the first time they go, but they keep coming back because they find friends there.

For example, Norm walks in the room and everyone in the bar yells cheerfully, "Norm!" as he makes his way to his favorite stool. Several interesting and colorful people made the Boston pub a home away from home. We all got to know the egotistical womanizing bar owner Sam, the sarcastic waitress Carla, the know-it-all letter carrier Cliff Claven, the not-so-bright bartenders Coach and Woody, the self-important psychiatrist Frazier, and the drama queen Diane. These people became our "friends," and for several years we welcomed them into our own homes at least once a week. Many of us still watch the reruns!

As their theme song says, there's something special about being in a place where we are known, where we find people who are glad to see us and get to know those who have the same struggles. There's something about having somewhere to go where we can put all the worldly pressures aside. Why shouldn't we model the church after this practice? Church should be a place where we get to know each other and build on the friendships and relationships we find there, and where we can surrender all those worries that weigh us down—not to alcohol—but to God.

Barstool Lesson Number Three: We must share our stories with one another. For those lined up on the barstools, it isn't unusual to hear people sharing their struggles, heartaches, misfortunes, losses, defeats, and their victories with one another. This isn't just Christ's desire for us—it's His law.

Carry each other's burdens and in this way, you will fulfill the law of Christ (Gal. 6:2 NIV).

But for some reason, we tend to cover up and hide our struggles and weaknesses in front of our Christian brothers and sisters when they should be the ones we trust the most. Some of the greatest stories of triumph and defeat are shared among the circle of friends at the local bar. Shouldn't it be the same or even more so within the church?

Oh, what a beautiful portrayal of Christ's love if our church communities were overflowing with dialogues of pain and struggle because people felt the freedom to expose their individual weaknesses. In the midst of those priceless and precious exposures of our personal stories, the purest essence of the redemption story is unveiled. The world needs to see that we are different. Showing our humanness and vulnerabilities will also show the lost that we are not the "elite" who have it all together. We are all in need of a Savior—from the lowest sinner to the most acclaimed pastor and teacher.

Theology doesn't do any good unless you put it in practice. Within this past year especially, I believe Mission Abilene has stepped out in faith and embraced this "barstool theology" wholeheartedly. We've become very open with our struggles and our stories. We strive to be a place where people "wanna be." We see people greeting and meeting and spending time together as they never have before. People are connecting heart to heart and building each other up as they share their stories. Lives are being changed. We hosted two new annual outreach events last year that focused on the gospel message through the sharing of stories and testimonies. The impact within the church and in the community was amazing.

Our Stop the Violence Rally featured speakers in our church and in our community who had been victims of crime and offenders whose lives have been radically changed by grace. These people found their voice and the courage to speak up so that others would also take a stand against violence in our community.

Our women's "Something Beautiful" Extreme Weekend featured speakers who had faced overwhelming circumstances and not only survived but found beauty in their brokenness through grace. They taught other hurting women that they are not defined by their appearance or their circumstances, but rather by who they are in the eyes of Christ.

In sharing our own stories with each other, we have given strong voices to those who were once too afraid to speak because they felt so alone in their struggles. All of us have found support through love, acceptance, and grace. We found family here in a place where everybody knows our names and are always glad we came.

Home Where You Belong

Joseph is one of the young men who shared his story at our Stop the Violence Rally. Just twenty-six years old, he is an unlikely serving member of any traditional church, even ours. He has already spent a lifetime of crime as part of the Mafia, involved in drug marketing and violent behavior. Raised by a single working mom, Joseph had too much freedom and got entangled in crime in his early teen years. The Mafia was all that he knew. He lived and enjoyed gangster life, making thousands of dollars each week with thrill and excitement at his beck and call. He was a user and manipulator of people, and he lived the lifestyle. Money, booze, women, you name it—all were abundant and freefloating in his life. The world was at his feet...at least until he got arrested for selling cocaine to an undercover cop. Suddenly his self-made kingdom crumbled. Joseph's so-called friends seemed to disappear—they no longer "had his back." He was convicted and sent to prison.

When he was released from prison on parole, he had to be accountable for his every move. He realized he could no longer live the gangster lifestyle. He never had to do life like this before—on his own, without money or the notoriety of the Mafia. Suddenly he was a nobody with nothing—no money, no name, nothing to fall back on. And his criminal record followed him everywhere he went. For the first time, Joseph had to live by the rules or go back to jail. He had to stay away from his old lifestyle so that he wouldn't be drawn back to it. He came straight to Abilene when he was placed in a halfway house. For the first time in his whole life, he had to fend for himself—no one had his back.

One night late at the halfway house where he lived, Joseph and some other housemates were discussing life, politics, faith, and religion. Erik said, "Hey Joseph! Why don't you go to church with me? I think you might like it. This one's different from other churches."

Joseph agreed, thinking, "What do I have to lose?"

I remember the first time I met him. He and Erik walked toward me outside the building pointing and laughing at me. As you can see, my congregation is really good for my self-esteem! Erik laughed saying, "See! I told ya, man! This is my pastor."

Joseph looked a little uncomfortable. Church was definitely not his gig, but he was curious and stayed. He found something here that he couldn't explain—a place to belong. Just a few weeks afterward, against our protests, he went back to the city where his old life remained—the life his old Mafia brothers literally kept calling him back to. He had to face them—to stand up to them. The Mafia "bosses" offered him thousands of dollars in cash, drugs, guns, power, prestige, anything he could possibly want—anything the old Joseph could possibly want, that is. They didn't like to lose; to them, Joseph's place was with the Mafia. He looked at all that he was offered and even considered it, but he finally shook his head and walked away from it all. Those things suddenly didn't mean so much to him any more. He had a better offer in a little church in the little town of Abilene. The Mafia was offering bondage and slavery as a way of life. Mission Abilene, his new family, and the Christ we represent offered him real freedom through grace.

The Mafia dads didn't appreciate his refusal. Their men beat him badly and left him in the streets, battered and bruised with a broken cheekbone. He still doesn't know why they didn't kill him except for God's divine protection. His immediate reaction—his old nature—was to gather some of his old buddies and take revenge, but as he scrolled to their numbers on his phone, he saw my name first and remembered why he refused his old life. He called me and told me he was in trouble. A friend of mine who lives in that area picked him up and gave him a safe place until we could get him back "home." He took a horrible beating, but today, he would still say it was worth it.

Joseph is still with us today at the Mission. He serves where he can, which is usually out of his comfort zone, but God is truly using him and teaching him at the same time. He still struggles with his old ways and his old nature, but he's growing. We have discovered that his "tough guy" image was just a plastic cover—there's a real heart beating inside, one that's been broken and bruised. His journey toward Christ has been gradual and often more than a little frustrating. He's still giving up that Mafia "tough guy" pride to become the man God wants him to be.

Day by day, Joseph is changing—his heart, his lifestyle, his values, and his trust in Jesus Christ. He never had to work a real job before, especially for a pittance in wages—that's been really tough on his ego. Nowadays, he is still struggling to find the right job that suits him. Silk designer shirts have been replaced by bargain basement oxford collars and off-the-rack slacks or jeans. Gourmet meals have been traded for ramen noodles. He's learning to pinch pennies and cut corners to survive, but he's making it—sometimes one step forward, two steps back, and then a huge leap forward again.

Today his new life is a challenge, and his walk isn't perfect. He falls down but he gets back up, and sometimes we have to drag him back up. He has Christian brothers who truly want the best for him and help him get back on track—he's finally beginning to learn what that "best" is. When he messes up, he knows he can turn to us. He's found what it really means for someone to truly have your back. We help him but we also hold him accountable—that's what real love does.

Sometimes we forget what we take for granted—what is normal for us has never been a way of life for Joseph. We've definitely had our ups and downs with him but every time he falls, we gently but firmly get him back on track. Joseph is learning to appreciate the value of a hard-earned dollar and to invest time in others. He shared his story and the first leg of his journey at our first Stop the Violence Rally. It was a new beginning for him and for us. What a huge step for him! He took his stand against his past and it was a huge blessing for us. Like the others who told their stories that day, Joseph gave a voice to so many others who have been too afraid to speak or who felt too alone in their own struggle. He gave hope to others who dream of leaving a dangerous lifestyle.

His journey has just begun and he still has such a long, long way to go, but his story is still valuable and still used by God. He's a man in the making—you know, just like a king named David was. He wasn't perfect by any means, but a man after God's own heart. This is the difference—Joseph doesn't walk alone. He's learning to make better choices, and we've all definitely been challenged; but we are family and he is one of us.

We're his "cheers" and I mean that more literally than figuratively. We pray, we invest our time and our hearts, and we love at all costs. Everybody here knows his name, everybody cheers him on. We know his past, we know his heart, and we give him hope for his future. He's sometimes tempted to go back when life gets tough, but he always gets back to this: No matter what his past has been, what choices he makes, he still has a place—a family—where he belongs.

STUDY QUESTIONS

1. Be honest. In what ways as a church leader have you unfairly judged those you have been called to love and inspire?

2. How are you specifically creating an atmosphere that welcomes and relaxes the average stranger who attends your church?

3. In what ways are you purposefully getting to know the people that walk through the doors of your church?

4. Are you and your church taking proactive steps in a greater effort to accept others as Christ accepts them and love as He loves? Describe.

5. In what ways are you urging the people in your church community to share their stories with one another?

Chapter 6

What's the Difference?

BEYOND CHARITY TO POSITIVE PERMANENT CHANGE

This loving thing all sounds like it should be easy, doesn't it? But it really isn't always so easy. If we move beyond plastic Christianity, we truly become a part of the Body of Christ, His church. As leaders, it is our responsibility to do just that—to lead. We want to be a church that truly makes a difference, not just here in our community but for eternity.

We can start a lot of programs that seem humanitarian and benevolent. We can give money to missions, feed the homeless, care for the sick, and clothe the poor. It all looks good and sounds good, but are we feeding the same people year after year without showing them how to feed themselves? Are we passing out hygiene kits and sleeping bags to the same faces again and again without believing God can change their circumstances? Are we enabling people to stay in their drunkenness or addictions rather than lifting them out of the pit? Are we just offering a handout or a hand up? Are we truly giving them what Christ has given us, or do we stop short with the "stuff" we give them?

No doubt, there will always be those who truly can't help themselves, and we are called to love and provide for them generously and wholeheartedly. So don't get me wrong—we believe in meeting needs, in feeding and clothing the homeless and poor, and in loving addicts right where they are. The difference is that we love them enough to encourage them to live out God's full purpose. Christ has called us to do more for those who *can* help themselves—to lift them up on solid ground and walk with them. We believe in restoring broken spirits so that people can be whole again in every way.

Our commitment to the community is "Come as you are…Leave different." The love and mercy of God changes all of us, and this is where the difference begins between the church and the local tavern. We don't just sit around talking about our lives—we live them. We break the routine. We aren't content with the status quo because we believe in more. In the church, Norm takes his wife's calls, better yet goes home to her; Sam is not only faithful to one woman but also respectful; Cliff delivers his whole bag of mail; Carla, Woody, and Diane find what they have been so desperately searching for in all the wrong places.

In the church, each one of us gets off our stools and takes our faith to the streets—to everywhere we are. We have to *be* a difference to make a difference. We break routines; we take risks. We don't just turn on neon lights to entice people into the building. As members of the Body of Christ, we are called to be beacons—each one of us a light that shines in the darkness. We simply have to choose to shine for Him wherever we go and in every circumstance—even if it's not so comfortable.

What's the Difference?

At times, many of us witness injustice, we see unmet needs and watch as too many people walk past the hurting and broken. Yet we silence our voices, we make excuses and justify what we see by saying *we* can't make a difference. What we can do won't be enough, so we don't do anything. And as long as each one of us chooses to do nothing, nothing gets done.

Scripture says as "Each part does its own special work, it helps the other parts grow." We are all called to do something—to do our part. And as each one in the Body of Christ—not just within a certain four walls, but across neighborhoods and cities and nations—does his or her part, we can make a difference. We have to develop the attitude that "it's up to me." We do what we can do even if it means we have to get out of our comfort zones. If each one of us reaches out to another, we've doubled God's kingdom. We reach out to those people others walk past; we love the unloved; we look our enemies in the eye and share what we have been given—grace, pure grace.

If you look at Mission Abilene's Statement of Faith, we don't have a lot of rules and regulations and bylaws like many churches do. We focus on Christ, the Head of our Body—on loving as He loves, united in purpose and faith. We are His hands and feet. We truly do love people just as they are, knowing that we have a great big God who loves them too much to leave them where they are. So going beyond charity begins with me. Am I willing to get off the barstool and out of my comfort zone? We can't make a difference if we aren't willing to be different even in the face of our past.

Making a Difference

After I gave my life to Christ, it was a real challenge to live a totally different lifestyle. I found myself at the local theatre rather than a keg party, playing miniature golf instead of peddling drugs, at the bowling alley with friends instead of hooking up with a girl. I found whatever I could find to do to keep me in line rather than falling back into my old routines. Admittedly, there were times I missed the rush of my old life when boredom set in. One such evening, another Christian buddy of mine invited me to hang out at the bowling alley with a group of friends. Woohoo! All kinds of excitement, right? Well, I was seriously desperate, and at least it was better than sitting at home by myself with nothing to do. After a couple of games, I noticed one of my old friends from my past. We hung out together during my more rebellious days, and we hadn't seen each other since my life had changed.

Okay, this was going to be a little awkward, but I took a leap of faith and greeted him, "Hey bro, how's it going? I haven't seen you in forever!"

He seemed relieved to see someone from his "old" crowd, "Man, long time, no see! How're you doing?"

"Man, I'm doing really well!" I laughed a little because I knew he had no idea. We talked for a while—almost like old times…almost. Our conversation ended when he asked me to go get drunk with him. Yep! God was definitely testing my commitment one more time! Pulling a drunk versus hanging out at the bowling alley…In the old days, there would be no contest. I just shook my head and smiled, "Man, I don't do that stuff anymore."

That's all I said, but we exchanged numbers and I left the bowling alley, maybe to make sure I resisted the lingering temptation. The next day, my old friend called me, and I had the thrill of realizing that I had made a difference just by *being* different! My old running buddy was puzzled by my change. "Chad, I have to have the drugs you're on! You're different— you're not mean any longer and you even smile now! You don't even want to go get hammered—what's the deal? What's so different about you?"

"Bro, I'm not on any drugs!" I laughed hysterically as I began to come to grips that I really had changed!

"Quit lying! Then what's so different about you?" He was confused but persistent. This was too good to share over the phone. I wanted to tell my story face to face, so I met him in the parking lot of a local ice cream shop—seriously, an ice cream shop! And I shared the whole journey of my transformation with him. More than two hours later, with tears streaming down his face, my old outlaw friend asked Jesus Christ into his heart. There's no keg party, one-night stand, or drug deal that can beat that holy rush!

What about you? Is there something different about you?

An Undercover Story

For those of us who have illicit or shameful pasts, we have to sacrifice our past to walk the straight and narrow. But this message isn't just for the unrighteous—it's also for the self-righteous. You know, the ones of us who don't just walk the straight and narrow: we walk the high wire in the spotlight and take great pride in our perfect balance and showmanship. But guess what? Christ didn't call men to walk above the world—but rather to come down to earth and walk the trenches with the rest of us, right in the middle of the sinners and broken people. And yes, you might actually have to touch someone! Christ lived and taught among the streets—among the poor and lonely, the sick and the broken, the criminals, and the desperately lost. But to whom did He show His anger? He was angered at the Pharisees and temple leaders because though they lived by His law, they forgot to show His grace. God's law doesn't stand without His grace, and to teach any less lets us believe that if we are good enough or righteous enough, we can achieve grace. But God doesn't measure our lives by our achievements, does He?

No matter how good we are, we must still love others with no condemnation—to love as He loves us. He doesn't measure us by our goodness. So those of us who have been cautious to keep our distance from the rest of the ground-dwelling gutter snipes or those of us that have created that distance to protect ourselves, is there something different about us that will connect with those who need the love of Christ so desperately? I'm not trying to sound high and mighty myself, but I want you to see that's what makes the difference when we go beyond plastic Christianity—connection. And if you haven't connected, maybe you're still seeking and don't even realize you've missed something, like Nicodemus in the Bible. You may be on a high wire, but you're still not out of God's reach any more than he was.

Nicodemus was a Pharisee and a member of the Sanhedrin, the Jewish ruling council. He was influential and powerful—probably a man of wealth. People looked up to him, and neighbors idealized him. He knew the Holy Scriptures by heart, and he lived by the letter of the God's holy Law. Though many of the council had lost sight of their calling, Nicodemus was still a good and righteous man, careful to avoid all temptations and devoted to his holy calling. His heart hadn't yet hardened in arrogance like so many of his fellow council members. At that time, his colleagues were greatly disturbed by a man called Jesus who did all manner of miracles and taught a new way to live—a way of grace. This strange, idealistic man was a threat to their authority, and the Sanhedrin unilaterally resolved to stop Him. But to Nicodemus, there was just something uniquely different about this man Jesus, and he wanted to know more. He didn't dare voice his desire in front of the others because he would be rebuked and ridiculed. He quietly observed and waited.

Something in the way this man loved and taught others rang true, and Nicodemus desperately wanted to understand. He *needed* to understand.

He waited until the dark of night so that he wouldn't be seen and went to see Jesus undercover. "I've witnessed Your miracles. If You weren't from God, You wouldn't be able to do the things You do." Isn't it a shame that so often as leaders, we go to God in the dark of night undercover? We are afraid to expose our vulnerability or admit that we still have questions without answers.

Jesus knew who Nicodemus was. He knew his position of power, He knew of his education and understanding, and He knew the deepest parts of Nicodemus' heart. Jesus also knew the great risk the man had taken just to come to learn more from Him. This was a man who could be changed by grace. He told him, "You must be born again if you want to enter the kingdom of heaven."

Nicodemus didn't really doubt, he just didn't understand, so he asked questions that to anyone other than Jesus would have seemed foolish. Jesus tried to explain by putting the whole gospel message in one little package—words which most of us know very well:

> *For God loved the world so much that he gave his one and only Son, so that everyone who believes in him will not perish but have eternal life. God sent his Son into the world not to judge the world, but to save the world through him. There is no judgment against anyone who believes in him… All who do evil hate the light and refuse to go near it for fear their sins will be exposed. But those who do what is right come to the light so others can see that they are doing what God wants* (John 3:16-18, 20-21 NLT).

Nicodemus stole back home with Christ's words heavy on his mind. Change for some comes quickly, but for others change is wrought more slowly but just as surely. He couldn't share what he had discovered, for he would have been cast out as a heretic himself. "You must be born again…" echoed through his mind in the weeks following. No one else saw the gradual transformation in Nicodemus' heart—it remained still just a stirring.

Weeks passed and the jealousy and hatred toward Jesus among the Jewish leaders became more intense each day. Meanwhile, Nicodemus listened to the whisperings and took His teachings to heart. The other leaders plotted ways to get rid of Him, even tried to arrest Him, but the temple guards even believed Jesus' teachings. The Pharisees believed they were the only ones left to hold the truth, and they scoffed at the others in sarcasm, "You're stupid enough to believe. Do you think any of us would believe that rabble? You're as dumb as the rest of the Jewish sheep who don't know God's law like we do! God's curses will be on all of you!"

Nicodemus could stand it no longer. At this moment, he realized that Christ's truth had worked its way into his heart, and he had to stand in the light—to defend Christ no matter what the risk, "Doesn't our law state that a man has the right to be heard—to explain his actions—before he is condemned? Shouldn't we hear Him out?"

Immediately, Nicodemus was under suspicion as one of those Jesus freaks, and they accused him of it but took no action. Still, his life was forever changed in that instant—for better or worse—and there was no turning back. He had come out of the darkness and taken a stand for Christ. He stood in the light.

Nicodemus couldn't openly share his new faith because of his position. His life was still undergoing change, and to openly stand up for Christ could eventually be his demise. God was

What's the Difference?

working things out according to His plan though. There would be so much Nicodemus would witness and experience in the coming days. Christ's kangaroo court trial, His sentencing, the crowds screaming, "Crucify Him! Crucify Him!"... There was nothing Nicodemus could do or say—all he could do was watch and believe all that Jesus had promised. He had to trust that Christ would be King even if he didn't understand. He watched from a distance in anguish as Jesus died on a cross that was meant for criminals, knowing that Jesus was no criminal. Nicodemus was part of the governing council, but this was not justice and he was powerless to change it!

It was time for Nicodemus to come out of hiding and let his faith be known. It was time to take a stand for the Savior who stood in court for him, a sinner. It was time to show the world that he was different—a man changed by grace. He couldn't bear the idea that Christ would lie in a grave for the shamed. It was time for him to use his wealth and his privilege for God's true glory. It was time for Nicodemus to put his own life and reputation on the line for the Man who saved it—who showed him how to be born again—a risk made even greater because he was a member of the very council who arranged for Christ's death.

Nicodemus partnered with another member of the council, another secret disciple of Jesus, Joseph of Arimathea. Joseph was granted permission from Pilate to take Jesus' dead body to bury. Nicodemus bought expensive myrrh and aloes to prepare Christ's body according to Jewish custom. While the rest of the Sanhedrin were rejoicing over the death of Jesus, Nicodemus and Joseph were so grieved that they risked their reputations and position to give Christ honor even in death. They worked feverishly to finish their task before the Sabbath, but they lovingly and worshipfully bathed His body in the oils and perfumes, wrapped Him in linen cloths, and laid Him with dignity in an empty garden tomb nearby. They sealed the tomb with a giant stone so that none would defame their Savior any more. Who knew that three days later, the heavy stone would be rolled away and the tomb would be empty?!

Isn't it ironic that at a time when all those followers and disciples who had so openly professed their faith and devotion to Christ now went into hiding, the men who had followed Christ in secret and in the dark of night now risked their own lives and came out of hiding, exposing their faith for all to see? They had hidden their faith in fear of the same Jewish leaders they now stood against. So often today, we take our right to faith for granted, but Nicodemus and Joseph were willing to risk everything they knew just to care for a dead body! Placing Jesus in that garden tomb was part of God's plan—He had prepared their role in it. When these men became willing to make their story of faith known, they became part of Christ's story—a story that will be told for generations to come throughout eternity. I would say that there was definitely something different about this man Nicodemus, wouldn't you? He wasn't just another sanctimonious preacher or teacher. His story is undeniable proof that even the self-righteous can be used for the glory of Christ. What are you willing to risk to be used for His glory?

Fredrick Nietzche once said, "I might believe in the Redeemer if His followers looked more Redeemed." The Pharisees spent their whole lives putting on the appearance of redemption, but Nicodemus never looked more redeemed than he did when tears rolled down his cheek in grief as he humbly and brokenheartedly cared for Christ's body. Before that day, he would have never dared to defile his own righteousness by touching death—somehow it was shameful in ancient customs. He had been a church leader all his life, but he had never been a part of the Body of Christ. Funny, isn't it? Nicodemus dared to touch death, and he was given eternal life. He was justified and made righteous in the heart of God. (Nicodemus' story is found in John 3:1-21, John 7:45-52, and John 19:38-42.)

A CALL TO THE UNDERDOG FOR THE UNDERDOG

I have been given all authority in heaven and on earth. Therefore, go and make disciples of all the nations, baptizing them in the name of the Father and the Son and the Holy Spirit. Teach these new disciples to obey all the commands I have given you. And be sure of this: I am with you always, even to the end of the age (Matt. 28:18-20 NLT).

These words are what we call the "Great Commission"—Christ's final words to His disciples before He ascended into heaven, never to see them on this earth again. He commissioned them to be the church to the world, not just their own little corner of it—the light in the darkness. Just imagine! He took this little band of no-name underdogs and gave them the authority not just to carry the message of salvation but to make disciples of the nations. He has given us His light—His life—so that through us, He gives life to others. "In him was life, and that life was the light of men" (John 1:4 NIV). He used those men that no one would have expected could change the world. They were just average "Joes" with not much going for them—until Christ invaded their being. The dictionary describes an underdog as "a person expected to lose." Unlikely winners: that's who the Twelve were. They were men expected to lose, but Jesus made all the difference. Because of Him, their lives, their ministries, and their commitment to be who He called them to be changed the world for eternity.

How many times I have thought to myself that there is no way I can possibly do what God has called me to do. We are all underdogs without Christ, regardless of how much money is in our wallets, what street we live on, or what titles come after our names. The difference begins and ends with Him. Whether we are president of a nation, ministers of the gospel, or beggars on the street—we are lost and expected to lose without the victory that can only be found in a life with Christ. We are all unfit for the grace He gives, yet He still gives it. He takes what is unfit and makes us disciples. He draws us together and builds His church. He encourages and empowers us all to go in His name and share His story, not for our glory but solely for His.

We are the Body of Christ—we are the church, not just corporately but individually. "As each member does its part." Each of us is called to be who God has called us to be—to *be* a difference. I am the Church—no one else will do what God has called me to do. You are the church—to be a difference in the way only you can. What is that difference? It's this simple: "I have been crucified with Christ and I no longer live, but Christ lives in me" (Gal. 2:20 NIV). If He lives in me, it's no longer just a Bible story—it's my life; and by His grace, I am no longer an underdog. I have entered into His story. To someone on the outside of the church looking in, I may be the only Christ they see. You may be the only Jesus someone sees—the only Christ they've ever known. Do people see Jesus in you and me? We don't have "religion," we have Christ! He is the difference as we live out His story in us.

Together we can make a difference—you doing your part and me doing mine. As the hands and feet of Jesus, we don't just *tell* a story, we become part of it—we *live* the story before others. And now we invite others to be a part of His story: "baptizing them in the name of the Father and the Son and the Holy Spirit." And we all live His story together as we walk through the pages out of sin and into freedom forever.

The story doesn't end with the sinner's prayer—we continue

What's the Difference?

to grow and learn and become more like Him. His story continues in us and around us as we take the grace we've been given and give to others who are without Jesus and also expected to lose. We are underdogs to the underdogs. When one of us slips or falls, we lift him up. The church is made of a bunch of underdogs—people who would be nothing without Christ. If Jesus can use an uncouth fisherman, a murderer, a tax collector, a crazy woman, and a little boy and his sack lunch, I'm pretty sure He can use you and me as well as the people He reaches through us, and the people He reaches through them.

At the Mission, we say, "Come as you are. Leave different." He makes the difference. In Christ, we are all victors and His story goes on and on and on. Why aren't His arms reaching and His hands healing and His love showing? We are nothing less and nothing more—the Body of Christ. If those twelve ragtag disciples can do it, so can I. So can you. Together with Christ, we are His Body—underdogs except for Him. We can make a difference for today and tomorrow and for eternity.

The following are two stanzas from an unpublished song written by one of our members, Tom Copeland and used by permission:

Love the Underdog

I'm always running behind, just out of step, out of line
Always in the back of the crowd
Reachin' for the hem of Your coat to heal me.
I've been beaten up, beaten down, run out of luck, out of town
Would You touch me please, can You look past my disease?

If there's a chance I can run, if there's a chance I can fly,
I'll bring my heart in my hands, I don't even need to understand why.
I'll fall on my knees, fall on my face,
   stumblin' like a blind man into Your grace.
Jesus, will You touch me please? Can You look past my disease?

The Superman Syndrome

STUDY QUESTIONS

1. Describe an instance when you consciously reached out to someone whom society rejects. How did that person see Jesus in you that they may not have seen in others?

2. If your old friends met you now, would they see the difference from the person you were before you met Christ? Would they want what you have?

3. When you walk "in the trenches," are you inspired by what God has called you to do or discouraged by what you see? How do you connect with the people you meet there?

4. Have you ever hidden your true faith and convictions to be accepted by other Christians? Describe.

5. In what ways have you taken a stand before other Christians to be the Christ you should be to the lost?

Chapter 7

Ouch! I Thought It Wasn't Supposed To Hurt!

BEYOND CALLING TO HOLY SURRENDER

Lord, I believe; help Thou mine unbelief! Here, on this sacred day, in the dust before the eternal God, I cast my guilty and polluted soul on the sovereign mercy of the Redeemer. Oh, compassionate and divine Lord, save me from the dreadful guilt and power of sin and accept my solemn, free, and unreserved surrender! Look upon me, a repenting, returning prodigal! Thus, O Lord God, am I humbly bold to covenant with Thee! Ratify and confirm it, and make me the everlasting monument of Thy mercy. Glory to God—Father, Son, and Holy Ghost—forever and ever. Amen and Amen.[1]

John Howard wrote this entry in his journal at the age of twenty-four. At the time, he wasn't deep in immorality and sin.

He was a young man devoted to his faith who recognized that even at his best, he wasn't worthy of the calling God had placed on his life—a calling of which he wasn't even aware yet. He isn't known so widely in Christian circles as his contemporaries, John and Charles Wesley. He wasn't an acclaimed theologian or a renowned speaker or writer, but God had a plan and purpose for his life. Even as he surrendered himself to God in this prayer, he had no idea how God would use difficult circumstances to bring about His ultimate purpose. Five years after John wrote this prayer in his journal in 1775, he lost his wife. Only days after her death, he put aside his own grief and brokenness to help others who had been devastated by a catastrophic earthquake in Lisbon, Portugal. He booked passage on an English ship headed for Portugal, but it was seized by French mercenaries during the voyage. John, the other passengers, and the crewmen were imprisoned under hellish conditions. I wonder how often he thought of that devotional prayer while he sat in that dungeon. "Make me an everlasting monument of Thy mercy…" Surely this wasn't part of God's plan! Surely God desired more for him than this sorry demise! How could this be God's calling?

But John Howard trusted that God would use even this episode of his life for His glory. Years later, John was the instrument God used to begin the fight to completely reform the cruel prison systems of Europe. He changed the course of history all because at the age of twenty-four, he surrendered his entire life to the Lord without even an inkling of knowledge for what God had in store. He was just trusting God for whatever was ahead. I wonder if he had known what lay ahead, would he have prayed the same prayer. When most young men his age were sowing their wild oats, John Howard was praying to be a monument to God's mercy—a permanent tribute to the grace God had given to him. God answered that prayer in ways that

Ouch! I Thought It Wasn't Supposed To Hurt!

no one could have foreseen. He placed a calling on John Howard's life, and John fulfilled it.

God has called me into ministry. I may not always have a clear picture of what that ministry is, but I am sure of His call without a doubt. I just never bargained that surrendering my life to His will and His purpose might subject me to so much pain. But then I remember the price that Christ paid for me on the cross—how He suffered and what He gave up for my sake. It makes my own suffering seem so small in comparison. I want to be an everlasting monument of His grace.

Who?....Me?

A couple of my fellow pastor friends and I were sitting around a lunch table one day mulling over what causes pastors to burn out, flame out, and crash out. These days we hear of it so often. Pastors leave their churches or the ministry altogether for a variety of reasons: the desire to enter into another form of ministry, a confrontation in their congregation, battles with denominational leaders or church politics, burnout and discouragement, family and parental obligations, marital problems or divorce, and even sexual sin or some kind of immorality—just to name a few. As pastors and church leaders, we are not immune to the same problems and temptations everyone else deals with, but we are held to a higher accountability. And the truth of it becomes more and more evident as we see more and more leaders fall out of leadership. As our discussion unfolded, one of my buddies, Trace, pronounced, "Statistics say that one of us will be out of ministry within the next five years."

That's a sobering thought, and most of us don't want to admit how much easier it would be to walk away from ministry than stay. The truth is that ministry often hurts or beats us down. But I quickly and offhandedly replied, "You guys don't worry, it will be me." Those words have almost come back to haunt me at times throughout my years and experience in ministry. I often go back to the day I first told God I would serve Him with all my heart and with all my life. I never believed then that anything could persuade me otherwise once I fully yielded to Him.

I surrendered to God's call to full-time ministry in 1997. I was eighteen years old. Sounds noble, but don't misinterpret the word "surrender." Many people use the term lightly, like surrendering to God's call is a gentle willingness to give up your life without a fight and without looking back. That was not the case with me! When I heard God's call, there was nothing gentle or willing about it! And more than once, I've wondered why I answered Him. I fought with everything I had to run as fast as I could *from* ministry, *not toward* it.

I will never forget the day I first felt God prompting me that He had a plan for my life. I went to the retreat pastor and told him about the feelings I was experiencing. He offered his diagnosis, "Chad, it seems that you are being called to the ministry."

I laughed because there was no way God would really want me to be a preacher! "Pastor, I can tell you about drugs and alcohol and even what girls to date or not to date, but I can't tell you anything about God and His Scriptures!"

I expected him to chastise me and let me off the hook after I dropped that hammer on him. Surely he would realize I wasn't ministry material! But his expression was cool as ice as he simply replied, "And that is why you are a prime candidate for ministry."

I was totally blown away after that conversation. How could I possibly be a candidate for ministry? It's hard to surrender to God's call when everything about you (by the world's standards) says that it would be a mistake. I could easily think of quite a few reasons why I shouldn't be in ministry, or maybe I should say "excuses." I hadn't exactly been Richie Cunningham. My dating career was quite notorious. Alcohol, drugs, and risky behavior had been my highest priorities. Reading my Bible and growing my faith had found their way to the very bottom of my to-do list. Public speaking and preaching were definitely not anywhere on my "things I want to do" list, especially if it meant I had to give up my life for it. If God had asked any of my friends or even my enemies for advice, I would have been voted the one least likely to be saved, much less be a pastor! All in all, I wasn't worthy of His calling. With my history, why in the world would God want me to be His voice?

But look at who Jesus called to be His disciples: several uneducated fishermen. Peter was known for sticking his foot in his mouth. James and John were tagged as the Sons of Thunder because they brawled so much. Matthew was a despised tax collector, and everyone at that time knew how dishonest tax collectors were! Several of them were just nobodies by society's standards. This little ragtag band of brothers weren't public speakers, but Jesus taught them to share His message of love, not just in word but also in deed. These twelve nobodies changed the world in their own day and throughout time.

Christ has a way of taking the most worthless and incompetent of us and making us usable and effective for His purpose. I didn't want to believe it then, but as the saying goes, "God doesn't call the equipped. He equips the called." I didn't need personality, skills, or reputation: I just needed to be willing. I still don't quite get how Jesus walked up to strangers and said, "Come, follow Me," and without hesitation, these men dropped everything and followed. God had to be a little more persistent with me!

God calls us to do His work and accomplish His purpose.

Like me, it may be in full-time pastoral ministry, but it could just as well be that He calls you to be extraordinary in other fields. He may call you to share His message through social work, nursing, teaching, or even customer service. But when He calls, you better answer. You'll be miserable until you do! And if you don't think you have the "right stuff," keep in mind that the disciples didn't know much either. They were a rough and tumble sordid lot, but Jesus trained them, built them up, and sent them out. I walked away with a you-gotta-be-kidding attitude the first time He called my name, but God kept knocking at my door until I gave in. When God calls and we refuse to answer, He doesn't give up. He gently pursues us; we can't escape His call. God called me directly into pastoral ministry though I didn't realize it in 1997, and it was several years before I finally answered that call. God calls each and every one of us to be a light in the darkness somewhere—to be used by Him in whatever paths that He leads us down. But when He calls us by name and we answer Him, we can never turn back.

WHAT DID I GET MYSELF INTO?!

In *The Message*, Eugene Peterson shows us that all of us are called as He paraphrases 1 Corinthians 12:7: "Each person is given something to do that shows who God is…" Think about that with me for just a moment. My ministry should show who God is, and that fact alone can make ministry seem bigger than life. I can't help but imagine what Peter, James, and John must have felt that day on the Mount of Transfiguration. A typical day alone with Jesus, His most trusted disciple trio—Peter, James, and John—enjoyed their fellowship away from the crowds and busyness of ministry every once in a while. On this day, though, something amazing and unusual happened. Suddenly, right before their eyes, Jesus' appearance changed. He was more than just human—He was literally the chosen Messiah sent by none other than a holy God. An incandescent glow surrounded Him, and His normal clothes transformed into dazzling robes—brighter and whiter than anything they had ever seen. Two men of ancient days stood beside Him talking: Elijah the prophet and Moses who received God's law. (It's still amazing to me that Peter, James, and John automatically knew who they were without being told!) Could this be a dream? The disciples were stunned and not sure whether to be afraid or be amazed. Peter, uncertain of what else to do or say, had a bright idea, "Lord, let us build some memorials for the three of you and just hang out here forever! This is pretty cool. It's real nice here!"

And as soon as he'd said it, a cloud came over them and a loud ominous voice from heaven boomed down, "This is my Son, whom I love. Listen to him!" (Story found in Mark 9:2-13.) If that had happened today, people would have been calling the Ghostbusters! "Somethin' strange in the neighborhood!....." Now, I'm sure that God didn't just happen to call down from heaven every day, but the disciples had no doubt that the voice they heard was His. They didn't even wonder or question. The disciples looked around. Elijah and Moses had disappeared and only Jesus stood before them. Surely that was the voice of God showing them exactly who Jesus was! The significance of that moment lingered as they went back to the real world, even though they didn't quite understand all they had seen and heard. They would all soon endure unbelievable sorrow and troubles. But they knew this one thing: Jesus Christ was the Son of the Living God. And He proved that over and over again.

When we choose to follow Christ, we are signing ourselves up for a destination of peace, but it's a flight full of turmoil, stormy weather, and uncertainty. Once in a while, I get to go to that mountaintop with Jesus and experience His splendor. I won't lie—I'm just like Peter, "Lord, let's just stay up here for awhile—just You and me. Those people down there are hard to live with!" But just as Jesus sent Peter and his buddies back down to the valley, He sends me back to the earthly drama time and time again. I'm glad for those moments, though, because they remind me who God is and what I'm here to do—what ministry is all about and what it takes to keep following Him. As I look back on the path God has led me down since that day in 1997 when I first heard God's prompting, I can't help but realize that surrendering to God was not a one-time experience. In my years of ministry, I realize that my life has required daily commitment and recommitment, often at an extreme price. We want to believe that surrendering to Christ will be pain-free. When we make the decision to follow Christ, we think for at least a few blissful seconds that we are signing up for a life of passion and peace walking in His footsteps—our own Mount of Transfiguration when we see who God is. Oh, how those awe-inspiring visions quickly fade into reality when life and ministry proves to be far different than we expected.

Then there are those moments when we wonder if it's all worth it, and we try to pretend we don't feel that way. We may be pastors and leaders in ministry—completely devoted to God—but somehow we didn't expect the hurt and struggle that comes along with ministry. After all, we're on God's side! Surely we should be protected or immune from these deep wounds that others inflict on us. We try to forget or ignore what His call requires of us, but sometimes the weight of it seems like more than we can stand. All too often, those outside of ministry don't have a clue about what we go through. They think it's about a couple of hospital visits, a couple of hours of study and an hour or two of preaching or teaching on Sunday. Easy money, right?

Wrong! The truth is that pastors are just like anyone else—it isn't like we don't suffer the same temptations, hurts, and struggles because God's on our side. In fact, we often endure struggles and persecution that others can't or won't ever see. We follow Him to wherever He says go—we don't lead Him to where we want to go. And where He leads may not take us down an easy road. How quickly we forget that Jesus Himself traveled a road of extreme suffering, hardship, and even death as He walked the hill of Mt. Calvary.

Ministry is definitely not without its share of drama. When Peter, James, and John were up on the mountain in the afterglow of Jesus' splendor and holiness, it's almost as if Jesus was testing their commitment when He told them they had to go back down to the valley. Why do we do it? Why do I do it? Simply because God called me to it, and I am committed to Him. Why? Looking back, I realize how often that commitment has been tested, and I am more aware of what it requires: holiness. Jesus gave His disciples a small glimpse of the real thing on top of that mountain. Then He challenged them to be a reflection of who He is. A worship chorus echoes in my head as I daily pray for the strength and willingness to persevere, "Holiness, holiness is what I long for…what I need." Yep, that's it. Surrender to the extreme.

A RADICAL CALLING

If anyone would come after me, he must deny himself and take up his cross and follow me. For whoever wants to save his life will lose it, but whoever loses his life for me and for the gospel will save it (Mark 8:34-35 NIV).

This is total surrender for Christ's sake. Some of you who

are reading this may be hearing God's voice right at this moment calling you to commit your life to Him. Some of you will choose to accept His call and some will not. And still others of you have been on this journey for a while and are remembering the moment that God also called you to lose your life for His sake. In my own commitment to get beyond my own Superman syndrome even as a pastor, I strive to be open and honest about my struggles so I will be honest even in repeating this: Saying yes to God's call to ministry does not mean a life of acceptance and smooth sailing, but once you've said yes, there is no turning back.

Paul tells us that "God's gifts and his call are irrevocable" (Rom. 11:29 NIV). Did you notice how he paired God's gifts with His call? He gives us such mercy and such honor in His calling, but He recognizes the burden that comes with that call. I could tell you all about the "feel good" side of ministry so that you want to jump at the opportunity (we hear it so often), but in this chapter, I want to honestly share the burden of ministry so that you understand the gravity and full cost of total surrender. Though ministry has rewards far beyond human measure, it is also a life of sacrifice, pain, rejection, exhaustion, and humility. We get to go to the mountaintop with Him once in a while, but He always sends us back to the valleys to finish the work He has called us to do. This is not a decision any of us should take lightly because the stakes are so high. Will I save my life or lose it and for what cause? For this life or for eternity? What will you choose? This is the life of holiness, the ultimate fulfillment of God's purpose.

In our supersize culture of megachurches, we sometimes get caught up in the masses and numbers—the games of religion—but living out God's calling and purpose isn't about the masses that walk through the doors of any church. It's not a game—it's

Ouch! I Thought It Wasn't Supposed To Hurt!

a matter of life or death for eternity. Living out God's calling is about the few who are touched and walk away from us totally changed and renewed because they've seen Christ in us. It's about taking Him out of the church and into the streets. In reality, I can't speak for anybody else; I can only share what I've learned in my journey with Christ—in the calling and purpose He has given me. God called me to be a pastor but He doesn't deal in generalizations. He gave me a specific vision and purpose in my ministry. In total surrender and submission to His call, He has given me—and I have accepted—my own life purpose as a personal mission statement:

> God has called me, Chad Mitchell, to focus on the alley ways of life, to recognize those who encamp these areas and have been overlooked or forgotten by society. As I find such inhabitants and He uses me, I pray they experience the love that our Savior offers and in turn, the forgotten will help others find the same love that is offered to all of humanity.

This isn't my job—this is my calling. I am a pastor but I am not perfect: I am still just a man like any other with frailties and faults. God has bidden me to live out a holy calling. Holiness sounds intimidating and unattainable, but striving for holiness is not about perfection. It's about following in the footsteps of Christ. Jesus said, "Follow Me. Follow in My footsteps. Live by My example." It's not an easy task! How many times I've wanted to walk away! I've even tried, but God draws me back and puts me on the right path—His path. Accepting His lot for me is an irrevocable choice.

I will never forget another unchangeable choice I made in little league baseball game at twelve years old. It was the bottom of the last inning, and we were trailing by two runs as I dug deep in the batter's box. Oh, the tension of that moment! I had struggled to connect the bat with the ball all night, and I was determined to make that connection in my final chance at bat. I choked up on my bat and peered intently at the pitcher; I was ready. The pitcher wound up and the ball soared across the plate. Instantaneously, I sliced the bat. Crack! Hallelujah! I connected, forcing the ball into left field. I made it to first base. I zoned in, focusing on the third base coach—my dad. Believing I could be the hero, I forgot that speed wasn't one of my God-given gifts, and I made an irreversible decision. I decided to steal second base, even against my dad's command. I took off as soon as the pitcher wound up the ball for the next batter. Even before I made it halfway to second base, I realized that my choice was not in my personal best interest! The shortstop already had the ball in hand, eager and waiting to make my humiliating demise a public affair. It was too late to go back to first. I had committed to run and there was no turning back now. The end result was inevitable. No angels in the outfield or infield for me!

Fortunately, on God's team in the "big leagues," there really are angels in the outfield and infield because He runs the bases with me! Remember, He calls us and gives us mercy again and again. I may not have speed or perfect skill but I have His mercy! In the midst of His mercy, I accept that His gifts and His call truly are irrevocable.

> *So never be ashamed to tell others about our Lord…With the strength God gives you, be ready to suffer with me for the sake of the Good News. For God saved us and called us to live a holy life. He did this, not because we deserved it, but because that was His plan from before the beginning of time—to show us His grace through Christ Jesus* (2 Tim. 1:8-9 NLT).

Ouch! I Thought It Wasn't Supposed To Hurt!

As pastors and leaders in ministry, we are held to a higher standard of accountability. And we should be. In whatever purpose God calls us to, He calls us to live a holy life. So what does that mean? In Jesus' day, the Pharisees thought that meant living by strict religious law. They didn't allow for grace. Sadly enough, in some religious societies today, we often still do the same thing, even with the New Testament of Christ's grace in evidence. Webster's Dictionary defines holy as "set apart to the service or worship of God…acceptable to God."

So how did Jesus do it? He was the epitome of holiness. He was set apart, but most importantly, He was set apart and in the midst of the very people He was called to save by grace. He didn't hide away in the synagogue. He didn't live in a commune apart from the rest of the world. Jesus lived and dwelt in the midst of the worst sinners but He was set apart. There was something uniquely different about Him in the way that He loved and taught—in the way that He worshipped His Father. He was set apart by the love and the light that shone through Him. Though He was completely and purely holy, He drew people to Himself. Jesus was most holy in His brokenness—in His suffering and death on the Cross—but God used His brokenness for a purpose so that all of us could become like Him through salvation.

Our holiness should be the same. There needs to be something different about me that sets me apart from the mob and draws people to the Christ they see in me. And though I am not perfect as Christ is perfect, I still can be holy in the middle of my brokenness—my suffering for Christ's sake. Holiness is not something I have on my own or that I can acquire by my own merit. It's not about me, but all about Him. True holiness is when His light shines in me and through me—when people don't see me but they see the Christ in me. Paul said, "I have been crucified with Christ and I no longer live, but Christ lives in me" (Gal. 2:20 NIV). When I can set myself aside and push Christ to the forefront, no matter what humiliation, hurt, or struggle I have to go thru to get there, I can finally begin to strive for holiness—to live up to God's call—a radical and irrational life for Him. "Teach me your way, O Lord, and I will walk (and even run) in your truth; give me an undivided heart, that I may fear your name" (Psalm 86:11 NIV). No turning back!

A Radical and Humble Beginning

At eighteen, I had no idea what God had in store for me, but I was submitted to God's call, "Okay, I'm Yours, Lord. I'll do what You want me to do. I'll be what You want me to be." The days passed, and it was finally time for me to be licensed to minister. As I knelt down in the sanctuary, I will never forget the profound words that a wise deacon whispered in my ear, "Son, if there is anything else in the world that you could do that will make you happy, do it. If not, then have no doubt because you are called to the ministry."

With a half-grin, he gave me the thumbs up sign and walked away leaving me confused and speechless. What did he mean by that? Of course, this is what I want—I have extreme confidence! I *choose* to follow Christ with my whole heart. This IS what makes me happy! At the age of eighteen, I really had no idea how often I would reflect on the deacon's affirmation as I learned what it really meant to live out a calling from God in the days and years to come.

Back then, I was wet behind the ears and eager to get about the business of ministry. I began to volunteer in the food pantry at Love & Care Ministries. I soon became the children's/youth pastor for the Mission, a church that was born out of this same ministry. I was on fire for the Lord, and I would serve Him in any way that I could. Three years later, I was ordained and my title at Love & Care changed to "Associate Pastor." My life and involvement in ministry was fast and furious. I was serving full-time in ministry, finishing graduate school, and trying to maintain a dating relationship with the woman who would soon be my wife. My schedule was hectic but in control. "I'm getting the hang of this pretty well," I thought. Even then, I knew that God had given me direction in life and ministry, derived from these humble beginnings among the homeless and poor. God had called me to focus on the alleyways of life. I could do ministry this way forever.

Then a bomb fell and totally blew up this perfect little portrait. The founding pastor stepped out of his pastoral role in the church to serve full-time as executive director of the homeless ministry. The elders quickly approached me to serve as interim pastor. Once again, God was calling, and I realized how completely inadequate I was for the responsibility of this position. This little church was filled with people most other churches wouldn't even receive. I had never been mentored as a pastor—the shepherd of a flock! How could I, a twenty-three-year-old young punk pastor, meet the extreme spiritual needs of people whom the rest of society had rejected and forgotten? With all my Bible courses and education, I still didn't have what it would take for this kind of ministry! College didn't prepare me for this!

Like Jacob, God and I had quite a wrestling match. I finally gave in and found myself at the place of surrender again. And in that moment, I was thrown into a whirlwind that would ultimately change my life forevermore. I became interim pastor and soon completely surrendered as I became the lead pastor of the church where I still serve today—Mission Abilene. I have to admit I learned a whole lot more from my many unique encounters in the name of ministry at this little homeless church than I could ever learn in a classroom. Flashbacks of those early years in ministry cause me to laugh from time to time. We have a common saying at our church that still rings true today, "Only at the Mission!"

From the moment I first surrendered to His call, God began to mold me into the pastoral role. It's been a radical adventure and I've learned some extreme lessons. I didn't know much in the beginning and I can't say I know much more now, but there are two certain principles I put in practice in those very first days that I've carried through the years. They are still my foundation in ministry today.

The first principle is that the call of God requires radical and irrational dependence on Him. At every turn, every new point of surrender (of which there have been many), I've had to depend on God more for guidance in my life and ministry than ever before. When I am weak, He is strong. God works and speaks through me because I have neither the wisdom nor the experience to be a church pastor. The second principle is that, even as a leader, God's call requires radical and yes, irrational humility. I'm not all that, but God is and He surrounds me with people who show me who God is so I can do the same for others. I try to show them not a plastic, impersonal god but a real and present God who cares about every detail of their lives. In those first nerve-wracking days as pastor, I recognized my ignorance and immaturity. I didn't know it all after all, and I certainly couldn't do it on my own. I quickly surrounded myself with as many people as possible who had experience and were also passionate about serving the Lord. On this foundation, God—not I—began to build my life according to His call.

Ouch! I Thought It Wasn't Supposed To Hurt!

AN IRRATIONAL DEVOTION

You know, we've all heard that old saying, "Be careful what you pray for." Well, I prayed for God to use me that day as I accepted the pastorate. I didn't realize then how much I was completely dependent on the Lord in those first days as pastor of the Mission, but looking back, I can see how my devotion to Him has grown. I had to learn what my commitment to Christ would require of me. I wanted to do it all in those days, but there were some radical changes taking place in my life. I had a lot of stuff going on, and I had been completely and busily happy. I didn't realize that my life and my purpose needed some streamlining. The funny thing is that streamlining is a continual and ongoing process.

All of a sudden as the Mission's lead pastor, I was slammed with a lot more responsibility and many more obligations. I didn't know it would be that tough. I was still working at partnering my pastoral role with full-time service in homeless ministry. I was doing all the things I did before except now I was required to prepare a sermon every week. I had not realized before how much time and study goes into a twenty minute sermon. And suddenly a lot more people wanted my attention to meet their needs. Even more people were watching my every move. I had a flock of wandering sheep that needed a shepherd, and boy how they could wander! I learned very quickly that I needed to readjust and reevaluate my priorities—a process that still continues to this day.

Almost daily—if not hour to hour—I am exposed to my poor commitments. Whether it is time management, wrong priorities, or failure to recognize what should or shouldn't be a part of my daily routine, it is not unusual for me to have to move things around or eliminate previous commitments. A commitment is something that demands a great sense of allegiance.

They should be viewed as if you are playing "Texas Hold 'Em" and you declare you're "all in." My first and foremost commitment is to Jesus Christ, and I learned what it meant to be radically devoted to Him. I had no choice but to be "all in."

Jesus said, "For where your treasure is, there your heart will be also" (Luke 12:34 NIV). What a tough statement to accept and to put in practice! We can look at our checkbooks, our calendars, and our relationships and quickly find out where our treasures lie. One fact that really messes with God's truth is that many Christians today convince others to pray this magical prayer and then send them out into the lost world without really sharing the hardcore truth that our faith is not something that we can freely acquire. Salvation is free but following Him—being a true disciple of Christ—costs us dearly and requires some radical priorities. One of Jesus' most disturbing teachings has strong language. Before large crowds, He said, "If anyone comes to me and does not HATE his father and mother, his wife and children, his brothers and sisters—yes, even his own life—he cannot be my disciple" (Luke 14:25-26 NIV emphasis added). He really said "hate!" Wow! Now that doesn't sound rational at all, but we can't show the lost who God truly is if we don't seek Him first and let Him shine the brightest. We get it backwards sometimes and serve Him with what we have. But the truth is that if we seek Him first in all that we do, He will give us the time and provisions for all the rest. If I make Him my first priority, I am letting go and giving Him full control of my life—my family, my ministry, and my every need. He certainly didn't sugarcoat the fact that nothing should get between me and God.

An Irrational Obedience

We serve an irrational God, and He requires irrational obedience from us—no matter what He asks of us. In fact, if we have sincerely committed ourselves to His calling, He doesn't ask—He commands. By the world's perspective, His demands don't often even make sense. With obedience comes radical sacrifice. We sing those words "I surrender all," but we often hesitate or try to ignore Him when He wants it all—our wealth, our pride, our security. We beg Him to stop when He asks us to lay our lives on the line for Him. Yet no one stopped Him when He gave His life for us. We come up with all kinds of excuses even in ministry when we don't like what He requires us to do.

Time and time again, God has called me to obedience beyond common reason. More often than not, the price of following in Jesus' footsteps is gut-wrenching pain and extreme sacrifice. I could gloss over this part of ministry, but I promised that we would get beyond the plastic picture-perfect façade to the real thing. The truth is that the pain and sacrifice of ministry strengthens our faith and continuously draws us nearer to Christ when we have truly surrendered our whole lives to Him.

Christ has called us to take up His cross. In His day, there was no need to fill in the blanks here; everybody knew the significance of this radical statement. The cross was an instrument of a violent and cruel death. And to further humiliate the condemned, they were forced to carry their own cross to the killing grounds. The cross had no other purpose in those days. It was an ugly and sadistic symbol of execution. Today, Jesus' command would be like saying, "Walk down death row daily and follow Me." Can you see any joy in that? Jesus was not kidding when He pronounced, "If any one would come after me, he must deny himself"—forsaking all other opportunities and ambitions. He meant that there can be no sacrifice too great and no price too high to pay for the sake of following Him. In my own life and ministry I can tell you, He wasn't kidding! And it wasn't just my sacrifice. My family and I have made sacrifice after sacrifice to live out love. We've given up a much more lucrative lifestyle and ministry opportunities to serve in a church that reaches the homeless and disadvantaged—a church wrought with problems and personal needs, crazy drama, insufficient staff, and very little money! We traded 9 to 5 days for 24/7 on-call ministry, and personal ambition for God's purpose. And this was the easy stuff to give up!

I'm not blowing my own whistle. There are many, many pastors and Christian leaders who have made the very same sacrifices in the name of Christ. To obey His call, there are genuine costs, but if we want to get real with Christ and get beyond the plastic façade of feel-good Christianity, we must be willing to pay the price. We are called to *action*. This isn't some magical prayer that doesn't require obedience. Works do not lead us to salvation, but true salvation leads to work and sacrifice such as oftentimes giving up huge incomes, "easy" ministry, fame, and recognition to serve in a homeless church. That's irrational! That's radical! But I serve a radical Jesus, and that's exactly what He did. He had the knowledge and wisdom to be a temple leader. He could hold His own with any Pharisee, but He chose to walk among the poor and forgotten—the rejected of society. He built His kingdom on a bunch of underdogs! The difference: Whose glory do I serve? None but His alone. Jesus warned us of dangers and hurts far greater than even these worldly sacrifices.

An Irrational Faith

If the world hates you, keep in mind that it hated me first. If you belonged to the world, it would love you as its own. As it is, you do not belong to the world, but I have chosen you out of the world. That is why the world hates you (John 15:18-19 NIV).

Ouch! I Thought It Wasn't Supposed To Hurt!

I can't say that Jesus didn't warn us. Because we are faithful and choose to follow our commitment to Him, the very people we love and respect won't understand and could very well hate us. Even in His day, the message and ministry of Christ was misunderstood by those who criticized Him. The religious leaders who should actually have easily grasped the truth of His message, in fact, plotted to get rid of Him. Why do people say the things they do? Why are they so judgmental? Especially Christians! These questions have bombarded me when I have experienced the most troublesome and hurtful times in ministry—not because of unbelievers but because of the believers—my very own brothers and sisters in Christ! In these times of unrest, I understand the truth of that seasoned deacon's mystical statement that happiness wouldn't be found in ministry if I wasn't truly called to it. He was right. Ministry is often *not* a feel-good experience. I can understand why David, Job, and so many other heroes of the faith cried out to the Lord in tears, anguish, and desperation.

The loneliest time in my life was not when I spent nights away from my beautiful wife while on the road at speaking engagements and conferences, but rather those days when I wrestled with the decision to leave a Christian organization and ministry I had served with my whole heart for eight years. I had been offered another position with another community organization. I felt that the Lord was calling me to a new chapter in my life as He fulfilled my original vision and purpose to help the overlooked and forgotten find hope and healing by reaching out with love to others—to help fallen people climb out of life's pits. For days, I prayed for guidance, questioning my own motives, my discernment, and my lack of faith. After three days of restlessness, I received affirmation that this opportunity was completely from God.

We often wonder why Christians are painted in such a bad light and often undeservedly labeled as hypocrites. Judgmentalism, hatefulness, and unfounded rumor and gossip within the Christian community wreak havoc on the faith of the strongest among us and diminish the effectiveness of the gospel. Just imagine the discouragement of new believers and unbelievers alike who suffer too. Jesus Himself knew exactly what it was like to be betrayed, abandoned, falsely accused, mercilessly persecuted, and weighed down with an incredibly heavy broken heart. He suffered far more than any of us, yet He stayed faithful to the purpose God put before Him, loving no less and forgiving all those who stood against Him. His commitment to the dreadful task before Him never wavered. He expects no less from us.

I pressed on in the path God had laid before me as I continued as pastor of the Mission and began a new outreach through a community renewal program. Though I bore undeniable sorrow and pain in this time of transition, God continued to bless my life and my ministry. Those loyal brothers and sisters who stayed by my side through this struggle and have walked with me in other struggles that followed remain faithful friends today as they continue to serve beside me in ministry, encouraging me and passionately praying for me and my family in all that we do for the sake of Christ.

God has faithfully walked beside me in every step of my journey in ministry. Step by step in every transition and every change, He is shaping me into the man He wants me to be. He has led me through many battles and struggles since I left my comfort zone of over eight years. His original plan and purpose for my life has prevailed through every transition, and my passion for Him has grown stronger through every circumstance. His ways are truly higher than ours. There are so many things

Ouch! I Thought It Wasn't Supposed To Hurt!

that we can't understand with the human mind, but I have no doubt that He truly does work all things out for the good of those of us who love Him.

Eventually, God brought me to my knees again as I wrestled with new decisions and new choices. I sought His will for my life and ministry, and I reflected on the years that had passed since I had accepted the pastorate at the Mission. As I sat at my desk one sunny afternoon, I was stricken with the reality of how far God had brought Mission Abilene from very humble beginnings. Originally a backyard Bible study for just a handful of people, the Mission now served the needs of hundreds, and we were steadily growing each week. God had been so good to our poor community of the broken, rejected, and forgotten.

Even in my new position at the community renewal agency, I felt the stress of extreme busyness. I continued to care for the grounds of our local cancer center—a job I had maintained since my teen years and still do. I was the lead pastor and the demands of that ministry were gaining momentum daily because of continual growth. And all this was on top of my full-time position at the non-profit agency, Connecting Caring Communities. Suddenly with the realization of my busyness, I was faced with the challenge of leaving my full-time position at CCC to become the first full-time staff pastor of Mission Abilene, but the sacrifice would require some drastic changes for my family. More sacrifice was a tough pill to swallow. My wife had recently lost her job, so our income had already diminished a great deal before I began considering an even greater loss of income to serve full-time in a church. We would be taking a $25,000 a year cut in our annual income! Great timing, huh? Once again, God was calling me to irrational obedience. He required a radical and irrational trust in His wisdom, His guidance, and especially His providence. He had been so faithful to me—how could I do any less for Him? With a huge vision, a handful of determination, and absolutely no clue how He would do it, I had great expectations for all that He has in store for the Mission and for my family. Once again I was forced to make a decision that would dramatically change not only my life but also the lives of my family. Finally I offered my resignation at Connecting Caring Communities and became the full-time pastor of Mission Abilene. We have birthed nineteen new ministry outreaches at Mission Abilene and added a part-time staff to serve those ministries. Though we are still a very poor church—we went through a whole summer without air conditioning, struggled to gain financing to replace a seriously damaged roof, and endured struggle after struggle—Mission Abilene is thriving spiritually.

That isn't to say that I have been without tremendous personal, family, and ministerial struggles in all this time. Satan persistently tries to tear down what God has built. Pain and grief are some of the greatest costs of living out His calling. Our brokenness draws us nearer to Christ because these are the times that we need Him most. Pain and disappointment are inevitable, but every struggle is used by God to shape us and remake us in His image daily. He has persistently pursued me and drawn me back to my knees time and time again. I fall down in worship, seeking His will for my life, for my family, and for my ministry. In the midst of each and every trial, God has renewed my passion for His purpose and increased my faith. I am more determined to follow His call than ever before. I am amazed that when I am broken, He makes me stronger in those broken places. He has given me a radical and irrational love, and strengthened me with a radical and irrational faith that grows in every struggle and sorrow. I will trust in Him no matter what the cost, and my trials only serve to make me stronger in faith and in Christ. He lifts me up with His promises:

Ouch! I Thought It Wasn't Supposed To Hurt!

Don't be afraid, for I am with you. Don't be discouraged, for I am your God. I will strengthen you and help you. I will hold you up with my victorious right hand (Isaiah 41:10 NLT).

AN IRRATIONAL CONNECTION

Of course, Jesus also said that we are to love one another as He has loved us. It's one of the two biggies! So how does that fit in with His command in Luke? The key is that we love others with the very same love He gave us, not apart from His love. When I became the Mission pastor, I was suddenly in demand with a congregation filled with extreme needs—spiritual and physical needs. As a church that reaches to people from all walks of life, I found that I often had to be many things to many people in circumstances I couldn't relate to or understand such as addictions, extreme poverty, abuse, violence, tremendous grief, sorrow, and desperation. As a pastor, how could I possibly love these people the way Jesus would?

In ministry, it's easy to serve people and still keep them at arm's length. We still have compassion, we still serve, we still love greatly, but we want to keep that personal distance—to remain set apart. In a church like the Mission, people don't always "get" boundaries. They needed me to relate to them at their level—on common ground. As a pastor, I am held to a higher standard, but in reality, I am just as broken and imperfect and fallible as any one in my congregation. I learned that to reach another's need, I have to truly connect with their hearts and their minds. I needed to let them see that a very real Jesus can understand their deepest hurts. I had to make a radical connection, and I couldn't do that on separate levels.

How can I possibly even strive for a holy life if I'm not real with people—if I don't reflect the very same Jesus who walked this earth? We were given eternity because of a very real, radical, and irrational love. Jesus' most faithful followers witnessed firsthand the love that He had for them even though they didn't completely understand it. They saw His pain and His suffering for their sake. That kind of irrational love changed history. He let them see the agony He faced and the drops of blood He sweat as He prayed in the garden for God's will to be done no matter what the price. And He said that we should do likewise. I think this kind of unconditional Christian love is the root of true holiness. Napoleon wasn't even a follower of Christ, but he understood Christ's radical philosophy. He was known to have said,

> I know men; and I tell you that Jesus Christ is no mere man. Between Him and every other person in the world, there is no possible term of comparison. Alexander the Great, Caesar, Charlemagne, and I have founded empires. But on what did we rest the creations of our genius? Upon force. Jesus Christ founded His empire upon love, and this hour, millions of men would die for Him.

If I truly strive to be holy, then I must love as He loved and give as He gave. Just as He was vulnerable, I must be vulnerable. As ministers, we work overtime to keep others from seeing our shortcomings and weaknesses. But I've learned the truth that in my weakness, Christ is strongest. I have learned that to show who God is, I also have to reveal who I am. In complete openness and honesty, I can connect with another human being at his or her deepest need. In my own brokenness, I am most effective for the gospel. When others see that I don't just speak and teach Jesus—that I need Jesus—they can recognize and admit they need Him too.

Ouch! I Thought It Wasn't Supposed To Hurt!

As Christian leaders and role models, we often want to be such a perfect example for others to follow that we don't allow them to see that we fall, we break, and we hurt just as they do. We want to prove our strength in faith and we so seldom let our own doubts and weaknesses show. Over the years, I have often been refined by fire—I've experienced the heat of it time and time again. I could pretend that I was tougher and stronger, but sooner or later it becomes a burden way too heavy for me to bear. I need my God and I need the fellowship and brotherhood I receive from His followers.

In my most difficult personal struggles in and out of ministry, I have learned that as a pastor, I need the same access to the church fellowship—my family in Christ—as the other members receive. Some people, especially other pastors and leaders in our community, think I'm out of my mind to speak so openly about my own personal struggles. The criticism from close associates, mentors, and friends has been heart-wrenching. As I am open and honest about my own personal struggles and my need for His grace, others see who Christ is in me—that without Him, I am nothing. And they connect with that Savior. In our honest humility, Christ is lifted up.

I Will Choose Christ!

I lift up my eyes to the hills—where does my help come from? My help comes from the Lord, the Maker of heaven and earth. He will not let your foot slip—he who watches over you will not slumber; indeed, he who watches over Israel will neither slumber nor sleep.

The Lord watches over you—the Lord is your shade at your right hand; The sun will not harm you by day, nor the moon by night.

The Lord will keep you from all harm—he will watch over your life; the Lord will watch over your coming and going both now and forevermore (Psalm 121 NIV).

I have been about as honest and open with you as I can. Living out God's calling in our lives is not an easy task. We all have that mountaintop experience when He calls us by name and reveals His plan for our lives. When we say yes to Him, He sends us back into the valleys to finish the work He has begun in us. We couldn't possible predict the misery and the sorrow that often comes with the call to ministry.

Blow after blow after blow. Unrelenting criticism, backstabbing, betrayal, abandonment. All these are the daily life of one who is called to ministry. We are beaten, bruised, battered, and no matter what, come next Sunday (if we're a pastor), we're supposed to stand up, face the congregation, and deliver an inspiring message oftentimes to those very people who beat us up.

Pain is an inevitable part of ministry. Who knew it would hurt so much? Who knew "I surrender all" really means all? Who knew there would be so many sacrifices? Who knew that Satan would use both friend and foe to try to destroy what God is doing in us, through us, and all around us within our congregation, our circle of peers, and our community. Gossip, rumors, and misrepresentation run rampant, ruining reputation after reputation, and more often than not, the devastation is a result of beliefs that aren't even remotely close to the truth. There are no "excuses" for pastors—no "good" reasons for bad things to happen. Who would have believed that ministry would be so competitive? We should all be in this together but so many are fighting tooth and nail to be the next Joel Osteen, Joyce Meyer, or Benny Hinn. I'm not dogging other ministers. God has called them to serve in unique ways just as He has called me but so many gain fame and fortune by watering down the gospel, and Satan never gives up. He attacks us personally through our weaknesses, our families, and our own feelings of self-worth. Doubts, temptation, anxiety, fear, anger—they all can attack us, and with each blow we grow weaker until we fall in humiliation. The rate of divorce and moral decline in ministry families is sharply on the rise. We aren't grounded like we used to be—we get so "busy" in ministry, we don't even realize that we don't practice what we preach. All these things are good reasons to run from God's call. We all have a choice. We can run, but if we are truly called, we will not escape His voice. He will whisper; He will pursue; He will call our names until we answer.

I know this one sure truth: We have a great and mighty God who can overcome all struggles, who will meet us at our every need. I serve a radical Christ. I follow in His footsteps. He asks no more of me than He was willing to give Himself. I am honored to be among His chosen followers. I am so blessed to call myself a disciple of Christ. I am blessed beyond all measure in all that He has done in me and through me.

I will choose Christ no matter what the cost. In my moments of lost direction, hopelessness, suffocating ambitions, overwhelming sorrow and pain, I can appreciate the moments I spend on His mountain. In those most difficult moments, He calls me to the mountaintop and He shows me just who He is. He has given me a promise: He will make a way for me! I am not alone! He is forever with me. He has promised to strengthen me, to help me, to raise me up—to be my God! Because of Him, I can be holy. He has called me to be an everlasting monument of His grace. I will take up my cross. I will deny myself. I will follow Him wherever He leads. I surrender all.

The Superman Syndrome

GOD'S DECREE

For as the sky soars high above earth, so the way I work surpasses the way you work, and the way I think is beyond the way you think. Just as rain and snow descend from the skies and don't go back until they've watered the earth, doing their work of making things grow and blossom, producing seed for farmers and food for the hungry, so will the words that come out of my mouth not come back empty-handed. They'll do the work I sent them to do, they'll complete the assignment I gave them.

So you'll go out in joy, you'll be led into a whole and complete life. The mountains and hills will lead the parade, bursting with song. All the trees of the forest will join the procession, exuberant with applause. No more thistles, but giant sequoias, no more thornbushes, but stately pines—monuments to me, to God, living and lasting evidence of God (Isaiah 55:9-13 MSG).

MY LIFE COMMITMENT

Forgetting what is behind and straining toward what is ahead, I press on toward the goal to win the prize for which God has called me heavenward in Christ Jesus (Phil. 3:13-14 NIV).

1 John Howard's journals 1770, quoted in Frank W. Boreham, *The Temple of Topaz* (New York:Abingdon, 1928).

Study Questions

1. What recent struggles have you endured that others can't or won't ever see?

2. What steps do you take to cope with these struggles?

3. In your own words, what is your personal mission statement?

4. Is God calling you to irrational obedience? What does He want you to do?

5. In what ways do you use your shortcomings and weaknesses as a testimony of grace?

Chapter 8

Rollercoaster! Rollercoaster!

BEYOND STRUGGLE TO INDESCRIBABLE JOY

Clinching the security bar with sweaty palms, heart pounding, and a bead of sweat trickling down my face, I settle in beside my wife and prepare myself for the "great adventure." I try to appear confident and eager as I sit in my seat and listen to the laughter and excitement all around me. Inside, I'm doing all I can to quiet my uneasiness and dread. I don't want to do this. Out of nowhere, the clicking noise begins and refuses to be silenced as the rollercoaster slowly begins to move. It almost groans as the car lurches forward. Click, clack, click, clack! Screeeeech! The deafening noise wracks my nerves as my anxiety reaches peak level.

The rollercoaster makes a slow, steady climb up to the top of a gigantic hill—inch by inch. I can't catch my breath! I glance quickly to my left, and I see the ground falling away farther and farther as we climb to the heavens. My tension mounts as we approach the crest of our ascent. Time freezes as the weight of fear and excitement both consume me. The rollercoaster stops and my heart takes residence in my throat. I can't move! An eerie silence permeates the air as I vainly attempt to lean forward. Knuckles white, my hands grip the safety bar with all my might as I get ready for the stomach-turning descent.

I want to get off! My heart is lodged in my throat and my own arms are paralyzed, frozen to the safety bar. I watch the daring show-offs in front of me raise their hands high in the air in anticipation. Down we go! Second by thrilling second, the momentum increases as the wind rushes through what little hair I have. The train trembles as it relentlessly maneuvers the death-defying twists, lurching to either side with every turn. Faster and faster we go, reaching speeds that surpass fifty miles per hour. Those around me are screaming and laughing in exhilaration and thrill, but I'm still gripping the safety bar, thinking that I can't stand another second—I wanna get off! This ride will never end! Then, BOOM! We stop dead in our tracks. The excitement, the phobia, the adventure abruptly ceases. It's over and even though the ride has come to an end, my head keeps spinning. My brain hasn't caught up with the rollercoaster yet, and gravity pulls hard as I try to climb out of my seat. I can barely stand up because my legs are shaking in petrified weakness. I lean over to Ashley and say, "That was fun! We should ride that again!"

STOP THE WORLD! I WANNA GET OFF!

In truthful retrospect, I would be completely okay living the rest of my life without stepping on another rollercoaster ever again; but my wife Ashley absolutely loves them, and I ride with her so I don't look like a sissy. As a husband and dad, I discovered that dream vacations of rough and tumble manly adventures soon get traded in for Disney World. It's bad enough to go on vacation to hang out with a big-eared mouse for a week, but it makes absolutely no sense to me that people get so much joy from being yanked around at ungodly speeds and getting whiplash. But then again, even rollercoaster rides have their exhilarating moments along with the most frightening ones, such as when we reach the crest of the hill and we pause for just a second.... I mean, we're on top of the world then. It's a breathtaking moment of hesitant anticipation and fear. Even I have to admit it's thrilling. But then a breath later, we are speeding downhill at breakneck speed, jerked around on sharp turns, and climbing up to mountaintops only to be forced into another deep valley while hanging on for dear life. There's no stopping and no getting off. We're in for the long haul!

Isn't life and ministry just like that rollercoaster ride sometimes? We both dread and anticipate life when we take off, but after a couple of stomach-churning, gut-wrenching, heart-stopping loop de loops, we reach a breaking point, and we think we just can't make it anymore. "Stop! I wanna get off! That's it! I've had enough. Someone put a fork in me—I'm done!" Tell the fat man to throw the towel in the ring; I give up. I'm cashed out! I can't do this anymore!" Okay...that's a little dramatic but if we are honest, don't we all feel that way at times?

When the hurts, heartaches, and pressures of life relentlessly push us through the twists and turns, gaining momentum with each struggle rather than slowing down, we desperately want to get off this rollercoaster ride called life! We want our feet back on solid and level ground. Yes, I'm talking about life, not just ministry, and no doubt most of you have been there at least once or twice yourselves. We sometimes get the idea that just because we are surrendered to God in ministry, we are immune to the ups and downs and loop de loops when, more often than not, we are in for an even rougher ride. We don't want our congregation or fellow leaders to know that we face the same struggles and fight the same battles with our thoughts just as much as the ones we lead. I know that all too often these same thoughts have run through my mind when the going got tough.

Some of you who are not old but may be beyond the third decade of life may still consider me young and even inexperienced, but I have come face to face with many losses and unexpected turns in my own life, which have caused me to grow up extremely fast. In the spring of my junior year of high school and before I found Christ, I lost five friends in tragic circumstances. I lost two more friends within the following two years, and not one of the seven was over twenty years old. Their deaths seemed senseless and without purpose, and I knew grief far beyond my ability to understand or accept it. Back then, I thought I was invincible and had no idea that life's journey would be sown with difficulties and tragedies along the way.

Because they often have no known family, I have been called upon several times to identify the bodies of my homeless friends who have been hit by cars or trains. I've lost far too many friends and family unfairly through tragic accidents, suicide, and senseless murders. I've watched my father, family members, and my friends deal with cancer and illness, some beating it through surgery and treatments, and some losing their life to it. I have officiated at all too many funerals including babies whose deaths seemed all too unfair and untimely. Some people seem to think that since I'm a pastor, I'm sure to have all the right answers, and I take tragedy and grief in stride. In reality, I have often struggled with a sense of uncertainty and confusion as I've futilely tried to answer the question "why?"—not just for others, but for myself.

Life is unfair and brutal at times. It doesn't always make sense. Friends and family turn their backs on us. Tragedy, betrayal, and heartbreak relentlessly strike again and again. I've seen them all up close. I've seen godly people lose their reputations unjustly while the corrupt are lifted up and honored without true merit. And just when we think we're on the right track, unexpected events turn our lives upside down. All of us, even those of us in ministry, suffer with the consequences and are bruised and battered by the lurching twists and turns of life's adventures.

I've seen the strongest in faith walk away from God or even depart from their own callings because suddenly the ride was too rough and they wanted off. These days, statistics show that record numbers of Christian leaders battle depression and suicidal thoughts, health problems due to stress, divorce, addictions, and extreme moral temptations, yet the world often seems oblivious to what goes on behind the pastor's closed doors until shocking stories make the headlines. We as leaders remain in our secret shame and loneliness because we are supposed to be above reproach. Often no one is ministering to the minister, and he or she eventually becomes one of the statistics. Too often grief, turmoil, and life's unfairness leave us white-knuckling the rails, dreading what's around the next bend. How often in my own personal struggles have I asked, "Why, God? Why is life so unfair? Why is the world so lonely? How can you even bear to look at us in the middle of our sin?" These questions have weighed me down, and I have to admit I've occasionally pleaded for the ride to stop so I could get off.

PUT ON YOUR SEATBELT

One of the greatest myths about Christianity is that when you become a Christian, the rest of your entire life will be absolute perfection without turmoil. Just smooth sailing ahead! Nothing could be further from the truth. In fact, we are almost

Rollercoaster! Rollercoaster!

guaranteed a bumpy ride. Paul often warns us what a rough ride it is. He is the greatest apostle that ever lived—the epitome of ministry building and evangelism—but he tells us outright that we will be smothered by difficulties, confused, hunted down and knocked down. He never softened up the truth or minced words—he spoke very plainly, but we also have to remember that harsh truth was always the beginning of the statement. The warning was always followed by a "but"—not an excuse but a testimony to God's promise instead:

> *We are pressed on every side by troubles, BUT we are not crushed. We are perplexed, BUT not driven to despair. We are hunted down, BUT never abandoned by God. We get knocked down BUT we are not destroyed. Through suffering, our bodies continue to share in the death of Jesus so that the life of Jesus may also be seen in our bodies* (2 Cor. 4:8-10 NLT, emphasis added).

When tragedy strikes, people often say it is God's will—even pastors. I heard it too much when my young friends died. That statement tended to make me bitter against God or maybe against stupidity. I wasn't a Christian then and to think that God willed my friends to die was more than I could stand. I wanted no part of Him in all my grief and confusion. Now I believe that God uses the worst in life to bring about His best. The harder I tried to run from Christ, the closer He drew me to Him. I still don't believe that God wills to take young lives.

I believe the choices of man and natural circumstances steal life away, and Satan has every intention to use these trials and heartaches to undermine God. But God promises He will work all things out for the good of those who love Him (Rom. 8:28). He said "all things"—not just the good stuff but even the bad stuff—all things for the good of those who are called according to His purpose. We were all created with a purpose. Whatever it is that Satan uses to bring about despair, God can use to draw us to Him and build our faith if we let Him.

There is so much we cannot understand with our human finite minds. Why do men make evil choices? Why do natural disasters cause such devastation? We need Christ most in our struggles, but all too often, many of us depart from faith when difficulties appear. We want to believe that it's His fault or at the least He did nothing to stop it. We want a Pollyanna faith which denies that our choices, the choices of others, or the world around us can affect us. So we cruise along enjoying the beautiful view and trying to believe, "This is the day that the Lord has made, let us rejoice…" (Psalm 118:24 NIV). Then suddenly, our train plummets downhill; we see a huge boulder in our path and just as suddenly, we bank ninety degrees to the left, then again to the right, then whoa! Upside down and around we go before we climb back on top of the world only to plummet again. And life is going so fast, we can't even open our eyes anymore. We're just hanging on for dear life and screaming, "Why-y-y?!"

Look at the last sentence of Paul's encouragement again: "through suffering, our bodies continue to share in the death of Jesus **so that the life of Jesus may also be seen** in our bodies" (emphasis added). Christ loved us so much that He gave His very own life for us along with the freedom to choose to accept His sacrifice or to choose our own way. Because the world is imperfect since Eden, we will all suffer whether we choose to receive Him or not. But in accepting Christ, our suffering becomes His, and His suffering becomes ours as we become one with Him. Our sorrow is His sorrow, our humiliation is His humiliation, our struggle is His struggle, but our defeat becomes His victory—windows through which Christ can shine His grace for all to see. His power and His presence are revealed in

Rollercoaster! Rollercoaster!

us and through us as we travel every hill and valley, every twist and turn in the track. We can ride hands free and high in the air, confident that He will make a way for us...even in suffering.

That's still a hard concept to follow, isn't it? God wills that all people would obey but He gave us a choice. Some of us simply don't choose to obey. We suffer from the consequences of our own sin and doubt but even then, we still have another chance to trust Him. Sometimes we suffer innocently from the sins and crimes of others and even then, it was a person's choice that brings harm, not God's will. In loving us so much that He gave us the freedom to love Him back, we sometimes are forced to suffer the consequences of another person's evil choice. It's not God's will and not God's fault! Let me reiterate: *not* God's will and *not* God's fault, but He can still redeem our suffering. It was unfair that I lost seven friends so young in life, but their deaths were neither God's will nor God's fault. God used my grief over them to draw me to Him, even though it meant He was in for a tough fight. Why? Because it was surely God's will that I should follow Him, and He didn't give up on me. He laid out the track and He steered me on course. Finally, I was strapped in and ready for His new adventure, without even having a clue what was ahead of me.

We hop in a rollercoaster with the intention of traveling at high velocity and put our lives on the line for a five-minute adventure depending only on gravity and a one-inch bar or narrow belt across our chest to hold us in. That measly safety measure doesn't look like much, but we do it anyway, don't we for the thrill! So why don't we just as easily put our lives in complete trust to Christ? He is our most secure safety belt in life. We struggle harder to trust the God of the universe than we do a metal, man-made strap! We want to read the map, tinker with the engineering, and keep our hands on a safety brake to stop when we want off. Even with all His promises inspected, double-checked, and proven again and again through history, we are afraid of trusting Him as much as I'm still afraid of amusement park rollercoasters…maybe more!

Trust God from the bottom of your heart; don't try to figure out everything on your own. Listen for God's voice in everything you do, everywhere you go; ***he's the one who will keep you on track*** (Prov. 3:5-6 MSG, emphasis added).

So often we try to drive the train ourselves when the track has already been laid out for us. All we have to do is buckle up with Christ, let Him guide the rails, and enjoy the ride. We have to trust Him for what we can't see. Christ never promised us that this world would be easy. It wouldn't be an adventure if life didn't have some ups and downs and turnarounds, but He does promise to be with us through every valley, every turn, and every loop. No matter what's coming around the next bend, by faith He will keep us on track. With each new twist, our faith becomes stronger. He is our guarantee that under His protection, we won't derail. He promised that He will work all things out for our ultimate good—if not on earth, He'll give us our reward in eternity. My aunt and uncle have a plaque that has hung in their house for years that states, "This world may not pay you much, but the retirement plan is out of this world." It may be a little cheesy but it's also true. There's more to life than meets the eye, but strap yourself in—Christ as your safety belt—hands in the air and scream for joy! But it's going to be a bumpy ride!

A Ride No One Else Wants To Take

When we think our going gets too tough, we can reflect on Mary's predicament just over 2000 years ago. What a ride she had! She was a teenage girl with her whole life ahead of her, happily engaged to a handsome carpenter named Joseph.

Rollercoaster! Rollercoaster!

Sounds like a fairytale romance—a loving couple on top of the world. Then without warning, their fairytale turns into a horrifying rollercoaster ride as their lives plummet straight down at breakneck speed. Mary was pregnant and not by Joseph, her fiance. In those days, good men only married virgins, and she was to remain pure until they consummated the marriage. How could this be? Purity was sacred and engagement was a commitment as binding as the actual wedding vows. She had publicly promised herself only to Joseph, not to anyone else. He couldn't marry someone who had cheated on him! The humiliation of it! In the culture of that day, the only way you could get out of this bond was by death. If a woman was caught in adultery, she could be stoned to death even if her indiscretion was discovered before the actual "I do's" were said. When people said, "I pledge with my life" they meant it realistically! But Mary was a virgin, no matter what people might believe, and she obediently trusted the miraculous promise that the Lord's angel had given her.

Mary was about to begin an unexpected adventure in her life—one in which she joyfully anticipated what God was going to do through her and her unborn child. At the same time, she fearfully dreaded the consequences she would have to face for her perceived sin. Just imagine! God called this young teenage girl to be the mother of the long-awaited Messiah! What a calling! But can you imagine what Mary must have felt when she had to tell her fiance and her parents? Times were very different and ramifications were very serious, yet she clung to God's promise. She was ready for the unknown when she made her confession. Who in their right mind would believe this crazy story that she was still a virgin and pregnant by the Holy Spirit?

Even though she was in obedience to God, by Jewish law Joseph had every right to either divorce her quietly or to have her stoned to death. Joseph was a good man and still cared for her so much, so he chose instead to divorce her quietly so that she would at least live. He was getting off this ride just as the train was leaving the station. And she still had to face her father and accept whatever consequences he dished out. Freefall ahead—no parachute! Her father could very well disown her because of her "sin."

At the last second, Joseph climbed aboard and strapped himself in this rollercoaster beside her. Safety bar in place, Mary wasn't taking this ride alone. He had a dream in which an angel convinced him that Mary was telling the truth and offered Joseph a third choice—God's choice—to marry Mary. Whatever dangers and freefalls, whatever twists and turns lay ahead, he chose to obey God and to stay at her side. Whatever the consequences, Joseph accepted Mary as his betrothed wife. As they topped the first hill, consider the ridicule that both Mary and Joseph must have received in the public eye. She was a fallen and shamed woman, and he was a fool to stay with her.

Even before they were married, Caesar Augustus issued a decree requiring all men to return to their ancestral hometown to register for a census to be taxed. Can you imagine the sharp turn this was in their lives? Mary was about to deliver a child that wasn't even his, and the law required that they both register in Bethlehem. No limousines or minivans for Mary! Eight months pregnant or more, she had to ride a donkey all the way to Bethlehem, definitely a bumpy ride for her! And probably a terrifying one for Joseph! He had never done this before either! What if she delivered? Neither one knew what to expect, and Mary's mom couldn't even make the journey with them to help because she had to register in her own city! Cold nights, back-breaking rides, and all the pains and discomfort of the final stages of pregnancy! When they arrived in Bethlehem, she was

Rollercoaster! Rollercoaster!

in hard labor, but because of the census, there were no rooms or beds available for her to rest, much less deliver her child. They were offered a stable—a place where the animals were kept, dark and dirty and probably not too fragrant. It wasn't really fit for a king, but at that point Mary just needed a place to rest. Scared, weary, and in pain, she probably very much wanted to get off this ride! But she delivered her son, the Savior of the world in that dark and dingy stable and He was perfect. For both Mary and Joseph, no doubt that was one of their "top of the world" moments. But there was no rest and relaxation for either of them. Shepherds came; wise men came—it was dizzying. They circumcised Him and dedicated Him in the temple where Simeon and Anna both prophesied who this Child was and who He would become. It was the first time Mary was told by another human being of the sorrow and grief she would face as a mother. Loop de loop!

Then another death-defying twist: an angel warned Joseph that King Herod had heard of the birth of the Messiah and that he was killing all baby boys under two. They must flee to Egypt. In a foreign country with a whole different culture and no family, they began their life together. This was not what either of them had ever expected. This wasn't fair! Why should they have to leave their homeland when they knew that their own son was the Son of God? They were strangers in a new land with very little to sustain them, but they survived and most importantly, Jesus survived. Finally, Herod died and they moved back to Nazareth. Readjusting, getting a home set up, a carpenter shop—did life ever stop? And all this time, Mary was raising a child who was wise far beyond his years. He was a normal child yet very different. He didn't quite fit in with the other kids. God had placed a huge trust in Mary and Joseph.

Then they lost Him during Passover when He was twelve—

no doubt, a stomach-turning, heart-wrenching descent for Mary! But they found Him there speaking with the leaders as if He understood far more than they, and so the proud parents topped another hill. At some point in the next few years, Joseph died, leaving Mary a widow with a young son—such grief! Joseph had loved her and loved her son so much. How could she go on without him? The twists and turns of life were many for this family.

As Jesus established His ministry, people began to reject Him and despise Him. To them, His talk was ludicrous and sacrilege! To others, it was life and hope and peace. Those people loved and clung to Him. He was hated and ridiculed, and plotted against. He was pursued by those who hated Him and those who loved Him. He was constantly surrounded by so many who wanted to hear His words and receive His healing.

These three years were an endless horrifying and confusing maze for Mary as she watched Jesus fulfill God's purpose. She experienced more ups and downs, twists and turns. She was on top of the world when they surrounded Him, crying out for His healing; but at the same time, the mother in her saw His weariness. She heard the murmurs in the crowd and witnessed the displeasure and jealousy of the religious leaders. No mother wants to hear words spoken against her child, regardless of his age. Her whole life had been dedicated to protecting and nurturing Him. He had grown up so fast. She was elated, her heart beating with pride and joy, as the crowds waved palm leaves and cried, "Hosanna to the King!" but in less than a week, her heart was shattered as He was betrayed, tortured and beaten, mocked, and condemned to die. She watched and listened in disbelief as He stood for judgment before Pontius Pilate and as those who had been His best friends hid in the darkness and even denied they knew Him. No mother should have to see her child suffer

Rollercoaster! Rollercoaster!

such agony! I can almost bet if she could have, she would have yelled, "STOP! He's my son! You can't do this! Let Him go! Let Him be!" But she couldn't; she could only look on helplessly as He painfully carried His own cross up a hill, still bleeding from beatings. She was inconsolable as Roman soldiers nailed Him to a cross and raised Him up to die an agonizing death...to hear His last tortured breath and dying words, "I commend My Spirit." She had to give up her son so He could save the world. Her ride of motherhood had ended tragically. Oh, but three days later....

THE MAN BEHIND THE CURTAIN!

How many women would really want to walk in Mary's shoes? At Christmas, we portray her life so beautifully, but we easily forget the incredible hardships both she and Joseph faced in all that God had required of them. We look past all that she suffered as a witnessing and helpless mother. Yet both Joseph and Mary persevered through their struggles because they were obedient to finish what God had called each one to do. Through the struggles and heartache, we see foremost who God is. He is revealed in and through her even in the worst of times.

Real faith is tested by our response to the unexpected. Mary and Joseph both faced the unexpected since the beginning of their journey together. Neither could have ever anticipated their experiences, which would have tested the strongest among us. If nothing else is gained through our suffering, if there is no other reason to press on through difficulties and hard times, we have to remember what the Christian life is all about—not about us and all about Him.

He [Christ] *is the image of the invisible God, the firstborn over all creation. For by him all things were created: things in heaven and on earth, visible and invisible, whether thrones or powers or rulers or authorities; all things were created by him and for him. He is before all things, and in him all things hold together...* (Col. 1:15-17 NIV).

"In him, all things hold together..." Do you remember the wizard's big ominous voice in the "Wizard of Oz" saying "Don't look at the man behind the curtain"? That gentle little man who had such a tremendous heart spent so much time trying to hide who he really was so he made up an image of an all-powerful wizard that could keep people shaking in their boots. As leaders in ministry, don't we often do the same? Well, maybe we don't keep people shaking in their boots... But we want to keep our flock in awe of us so that they can rise above their own hurts and temptations through our spotless example. We want them to think we have it all figured out so we create an image that's above reproach. But God desperately wants to reveal His true self to us, in us, and through us. He wants us to know that He is our Designer, the Creator of the Universe, the Alpha and Omega, the Author of every story, the Name above all names and He proves Himself time and again through our struggles. In our ups as we rejoice, in our downs as we freefall to bottomless pits of sorrow and grief, and in every loop de loop and twist and turn flying at breakneck speeds as we continuously put our lives in trust to the greatest security belt, Jesus Christ. No matter what comes our way, He holds us together. We can persevere.

The greatness of God's character—His all-consuming strength and power, His never ending mercy, His ever present love and gentleness—is best displayed through the testimonies of those who have persevered and overcome the worst that life

Rollercoaster! Rollercoaster!

can throw at them. Paul said it best when he shared God's response after he begged three times for God to take away his struggles:

Each time He said, "My grace is all you need. My power works best in weakness." So now I am glad to boast about my weaknesses, so that the power of Christ can work through me. That's why I take pleasure in my weaknesses, and in the insults, hardships, persecutions, and troubles that I suffer for Christ. For when I am weak, then I am strong (2 Cor. 12:9-10 NLT).

When we are the weakest, He is the strongest. When we can't do anything, God can do everything. In the midst of struggle, we often come face to face with our own weakness, and it's in these times that even the most stubborn of us have to surrender all to rely on His strength. And just maybe, if we are more honest and real with the people we serve, they will actually relate more and grow because they know that we battle the same battles. We tend to give Him the most room to do His best work when we have thrown our hands up and given up. Then He can do things that we could never do on our own. And we are so breathless when He is done that we can't say anything but give Him the glory for it. What a ride!

RISKS, RULES, AND RECOMMENDATIONS

Okay, so are you ready to roll? Let's talk a little bit about how you can make it to the end without tossing your cookies. After all, every amusement park ride has posted signs that advise potential passengers of the risks, rules, and recommendations to get the most enjoyment from the ride experience. So maybe we should take a look at a few of those for some helpful hints for your own rollercoaster adventure. You know, those advisements like "Please keep all your body limbs and personal articles in the vehicle at all times." Remember, I'm a stickler for that one—hands always on the security bar!

Or this one: "Please do not exit the vehicle until the ride has completed and the attendant has unlocked your seatbelts." You have to wonder what prompts some of these warnings. Some of them are just plain common sense or so you would think! Some clown must have decided to get out and take his own route to the end for that rule to be posted! In the ride of life, it's the foremost warning reminding us to hang in there until the end. The key is perseverance. Before you even get in, you've got to make up your mind to ride it out to the finish. To persevere is to "persist in anything undertaken; maintain a purpose in spite of difficulty, obstacles, or discouragement; continue steadfastly." Life is an unstoppable ride; once you're moving, you can't get off anyway.

One sign says, "Please secure all loose articles or leave them with the attendant." There's nothing more irritating that getting slapped in the face with your own cotton candy or tied up in your camera straps! Loose articles and unnecessary baggage can be dangerous, so that's sound advice before you even move out of the station! "...Let us throw off everything that hinders and the sin that so easily entangles, and let us run with perseverance the race marked out for us" (Heb. 12:1 NIV). In life, if we're honest, most of us can easily call to mind some unnecessary baggage that we carry around with us that slows us down, trips us up, and causes all sorts of trouble when all we need to do is put it down so it doesn't get in our way any longer. Life brings about enough suffering on its own without us adding to it. We hang on to the silliest things when Christ has already promised He will provide all that we need—He will BE all that we need.

Rollercoaster! Rollercoaster!

Another sign says, "This ride has been inspected and maintained the highest safety rating." Every year, Abilene hosts the West Texas Fair which includes various carnival rides. I found it interesting this past year that some of the rides had posted signs concerning their safety ratings, including how long it has been since there had been any accidents. Of course, when it says "This ride has maintained the highest safety rating for two years," I begin to wonder, *What happened two years ago?* But the purpose of informing the passengers that the ride has passed inspection and maintained safety requirements is to win our trust so that we buckle up with confidence. So before you take off again, has your life rollercoaster passed inspection for maximum safety? Has it been constructed and maintained by Christ Himself? Or are you putting your trust in second-rate architecture and engineering?

In high school, I assisted in coaching a Special Olympics' tennis team. I was a good tennis player so I thought I had a lot to teach these special athletes, but it turned out I learned so much more from them. The University of Texas hosted the State Special Olympics Tournament. One of my responsibilities as an assistant was to look after a couple of the special team athletes. On the first day of the tournament, one of my assigned athletes and I stepped into the dorm elevator with no doubt that we would end up where we were headed. The elevator door closed and away we...Well, I thought away we'd go but instead, the elevator froze. So picture this: I'm trapped on the fourth floor in an elevator with an athlete who has severe special needs. I calmed him and assured him that we would be okay. Well, that's what I should have done! Instead, my special needs friend was the calm one, and I went into a full-blown panic, my thoughts racing, *We're stuck in the elevator!* I began beating on the elevator door and yelling, desperately hoping someone would hear me and come to our rescue. We were rescued all right, but not by experienced technicians or even emergency personnel coming through the emergency hatch. That would be far more exciting and much less humiliating for me! No, my special friend saved the day. He said, "Chad, we might get out of here if we push a button."

Okay, so I wasn't always the quick-witted, intelligent pastor I am today! Well, I have my moments anyway… Sometimes I wonder how I even make it from day to day when I put all my faith in my own strength. Blind eyes, deaf ears, self-centered priorities, and self-righteous pride often misguide my faith in the wrong direction. I must trust in Christ to be certain my own heart is tested and proven strong enough for the journey—constructed and maintained by the Master Architect and Giver of life, Jesus Christ. "Let us fix our eyes on Jesus, the author and perfecter of our faith…" (Heb. 12:2 NIV). He is our assurance. Coasting on what Christ has engineered and constructed insures a confident ride. We can trust what He builds.

Finally, the last sign is the one I like the best, "Enjoy the ride!" Don't you love it when even a sign offers us a grand bon voyage? It adds to the anticipation and thrill of the ride. Why do we ride rollercoasters anyway? Because we like having our breath taken away. We thrive on thrill—the speed, the unexpected! And the thrills of the ride are worth the weak knees, churning stomach, and the thumping heart. At the end of the ride, we've forgotten the nausea, but we remember the breathless moments…the highlights. So often in life, we get so caught up in the trials and tribulations that we forget to enjoy our blessings. Paul reminds us that we don't have to wait until heaven to enjoy what God has for us:

Summing it all up, friends, I'd say you'll do best by filling your minds and meditating on things true, noble, reputable,

Rollercoaster! Rollercoaster!

authentic, compelling, gracious—the best, not the worst; the beautiful, not the ugly; things to praise, not things to curse. Put into practice what you learned from me, what you heard and saw and realized. Do that, and God, who makes everything work together, will work you into his most excellent harmonies (Phil. 4:8-9 MSG).

We persevere by remembering "the good stuff" when the bad threatens to take us down. Someone once said, "Life is not measured by the number of breaths we take, but by the moments that take our breath away." Isn't that so true? In the end, our lives are measured by what is true and noble, the best, the beautiful, and the praiseworthy. In remembering the good, we recognize how God is working our lives out according to His plan and that encourages us to keep our heads up. We can get through the valley so we can reach another mountaintop. Okay, now we know all the risks, rules, and recommendations: Let's roll!

RIDE FOR JOY!

Still have a few doubts? You're buckled in, the coaster is climbing that first hill, but you're still wondering why in the world you should put yourself through all this. Why not just sail along with the status quo? You only came along on the ride so you don't look like a wimp. I understand that—I rode with Ashley at Disney World so she didn't think I was a sissy! Well, Disney World's rollercoaster is just a five minute adventure, but now Ashley and I have a lifetime memory—an enduring moment of joy. So maybe the Disney ride was worth it. I love my wife and I cherish any moment that connects us. So it is with life. This ride is more than just a frivolous adventure; God has purpose for your journey. Remember, we have already focused on the Author and Perfecter of our faith, Jesus Christ, and we see God's purpose revealed and also the greatest encouragement to ride life out to the end as we read on:

> *Let us fix our eyes on Jesus, the author and perfecter of our faith who for the joy set before Him endured the **cross**, scorning its shame, and sat down at the right hand of the throne of God. Consider him who endured such opposition from sinful men, so that you will not grow weary and lose heart* (Heb. 12:2-3 NIV, emphasis added).

God's purpose is revealed in the Cross of Christ: "For the joy set before Him." The Cross is exactly where we meet Jesus face to face—where His suffering becomes our own, and our suffering becomes His. The Cross is our redemption—His means to a perfect ending or rather "unending"—the Resurrection—our hope for eternity. So there at the Cross, in His suffering and in our own, we find true and everlasting joy. It doesn't really make sense in our limited thinking, does it? Joy in suffering—what a concept! But in our suffering, we grow into who God intends for us to be. It certainly doesn't feel like it, though, when we're in the middle of our hurt, but we can be assured of this great reward of our struggle as it continues to work His miracle in us.

The beginning of that lifelong miracle is salvation—in accepting all that God is because of all that Christ accomplished on the cross. Through His suffering, His death, and then His resurrection, we can see that our heavenly Father is the Son of God, fully God and fully man. He knows us because He created us. He understands us because He experienced suffering beyond anything we can imagine. So through our adversities, we are refined and made perfect through His sacrifice. We rejoice in our salvation and in the working of our salvation as we are refined, so much that we can't even justly express the joy He gives.

Rollercoaster! Rollercoaster!

In this you greatly rejoice, though now for a little while you may have had to suffer grief in all kinds of trials. These have come so that your faith—of greater worth than gold, which perishes even though refined by fire—may be proved genuine and may result in praise, glory and honor when Jesus Christ is revealed. Though you have not seen him, you love him; and even though you do not see him now, you believe in him and are filled with an inexpressible and glorious joy, for you are receiving the goal of your faith, the salvation of your souls (1 Peter 1:6-9 NIV).

And still the miracle has only begun! Have you ever watched babies just learning to walk? They are so cute waddling around and eventually tumbling to the ground! The scene makes for a lot of laughter and Kodak moments. But in reality, they fall down because they aren't finished growing. Their bodies are weird and unbalanced. Babies' heads are far bigger in comparison to their bodies, so naturally they fall down because their heads weigh too much. There is not equilibrium and down they go. As growing Christians, we are the same. We have no equilibrium because we're still growing, and sometimes we fall down. Is that a reason to give up? Not at all.

When a baby falls down, does the parent get up and spank the child? Of course not! It would be ridiculous to punish him because he hasn't grown up yet! So why do we get so down on ourselves when we fall? Just like a loving parent, I wholeheartedly believe that Christ looks at us fall, hears our cry, forgives us, and puts us back on our feet to keep walking. After all, He was human—He had to learn to walk once upon a time too. The problem appears when we throw our temper tantrum, screaming and kicking our feet in the dirt so that He can't pick us up and help us to stand again. Even so, He understands and has enduring patience as we mature and grow into who God intends us to be. We grow through our mistakes and through our suffering. As a child grows, his body transforms and becomes more balanced. His legs grow long, his bones straighten, and before you know it everything is in proportion, and he can easily stand on his own. So it is with us—we find balance in our suffering and it begins with perseverance. We rejoice in that growth—in becoming all that God has intended us to be!

> *And we rejoice in the hope of the glory of God. Not only so, but we also rejoice in our sufferings, because we know that suffering produces perseverance; perseverance, character; and character, hope. And hope does not disappoint us, because God has poured out His love into our hearts by the Holy Spirit, whom He has given us* (Rom. 5:2-5 NIV).

And still the joyous miracle has not finished! The most powerful way to touch a hardened heart is for that heart to witness the genuine miracle in the life of one who has been through the worst and surrendered all to Christ. Our testimonies can impact others because we are living proof that God is real, that He is exists, and that He is present in our world today. As we reach out to others and use what we have learned to teach others, we rejoice in fellowship with each other as we walk in His light together.

> *This One [Jesus Christ] who is life itself was revealed to us, and we have seen him. And now we testify and proclaim to you that he is the one who is eternal life. He was with the Father, and then he was revealed to us. We proclaim to you what we ourselves have actually seen and heard so that you may have fellowship with us. And our fellowship is with the Father and with his Son, Jesus Christ. We are writing these*

Rollercoaster! Rollercoaster!

things so that you may fully share our joy. This is the message we heard from Jesus and now declare to you: God is light, and there is no darkness in him at all. If we are living in the light, as God is in the light, then we have fellowship with each other, and the blood of Jesus, his Son, cleanses us from all sin (1 John 1:2-5,7 NLT).

Have you ever considered how much light is a significant part of every celebration? For example, there are candles on a birthday cake or on the table for an anniversary dinner and twinkling lights on the Christmas tree to celebrate Jesus' birthday. Even in an amusement park, some of the greatest awe and wonder appears when the colorful displays of laser lights and fireworks brighten the sky as darkness falls.

Life's rollercoaster offers so much more than just a ride through time until we meet Him face to face. Joy was not just meant for eternity. Joy is meant to be lived and celebrated as we experience the ups and downs of life right now—in fact, such joy that we can't contain it or explain it! The King James version of the Bible calls it "Joy unspeakable, and full of glory" (1 Peter 1:8). Isn't that a beautiful way to put it!

STEP RIGHT UP! GET YOUR TICKETS!

We know the rules, the reasons, and the rewards for taking this ride of a lifetime that Jesus so freely offers. It's time for you to lead a contingent there! Step right up and get tickets for the most thrilling and indescribable journey. The engineer has a free pass for you and everyone with you! You only get to ride once, but He guarantees you perfect seats!

Christ offers even more than we could ever ask or imagine. We may have twists and turns, ups and downs, and unexpected loop de loops, but we still can enjoy it. There is no turning back and no do-overs. The best is yet to be! The most beautiful moment in life's rollercoaster ride is when we come into the exit gate and Jesus is standing there arms wide open, welcoming us into a whole new world and saying, "Good ride! What a faithful passenger."

I think that when I come to the end of my life's ride, I'll be tempted to bend over and whisper to Him, "Let's do it again."

> *Everything that goes into a life of pleasing God has been miraculously given to us by getting to know, personally and intimately, the One who invited us to God. The best invitation we ever received! We were also given absolutely terrific promises to pass on to you—your tickets to participation in the life of God after you turned your back on a world corrupted by lust. So don't lose a minute in building on what you've been given, complementing your basic faith with good character, spiritual understanding, alert discipline, passionate patience, reverent wonder, warm friendliness, and generous love, each dimension fitting into and developing the others. With these qualities active and growing in your lives, no grass will grow under your feet, no day will pass without its reward as you mature in your experience of our Master Jesus. Without these qualities you can't see what's right before you, oblivious that your old sinful life has been wiped off the books* (2 Peter 1:3-9 MSG).

STUDY QUESTIONS

1. As a pastor or leader, you spend most of your time ministering to others. Who is currently ministering to YOU?

_____
_____
_____

2. When is the last time you suffered the consequences of another person's evil choices?

_____
_____
_____

3. How did you cope with that experience?

_____
_____
_____

4. In recent days, have you suffered unexpectedly? What are your experiences?

_____
_____
_____

5. How are you currently using your testimony to impact others?

_____
_____
_____

6. Take off the Superman cape and be honest. What unnecessary baggage are you carrying around?

_____
_____
_____

7. How do you purposefully enjoy the "good stuff" God has given you?

_____
_____
_____

Chapter 9

Running Into "Happily Ever After"

BEYOND LIFE TO EVERLASTING LEGACY

You're sitting on the edge of your seat at your favorite team's sporting event. Winning is crucial because this final score will determine which team is to continue to play in the season playoffs. Your team is still a few points short of tying this game. If only they can score once more, they can still win. Two minutes are left on the clock, then one minute. The seconds are ticking away! 10, 9, 8…until the dreaded buzzer sounds at 0! Your team loses. The game is over and with it all hopes of a championship title. The season comes to a sudden and grinding halt. Suddenly all the chills and thrills, the ups and downs are all over!

As chaplain of the Abilene High School football team for the last several years, I've been on the sidelines with the team through their victories and their losses. Occasionally throughout the year, I cause them to pause in the locker room and look at one another just as they are in that moment. As each one looks around the room into the eyes of their fellow teammates, I remind them that they will never play another season with this very same team. Some players will graduate, some will move away, and unfortunately some may get hurt and never have the opportunity to play another season. But no matter what, the team will never be the same again. As I remind them of the obvious, I encourage them to become a team that will be remembered throughout AHS history. What this team can accomplish both on and off the field through hard work, courage, character, dedication, and spirit can impact future generations and leave a legacy of brotherhood for those who come behind them.

What about the game of life that we all must play? Why do we do what we do? Why are we in ministry? Why fight the battles we fight when it seems so futile? As our life clock counts off the minutes and seconds one by one and the final buzzer sounds, will we even be remembered throughout the ages? Will the people we helped along the way remember that we showed our Christian faith through our own courage, character, dedication and spirit? It may have been a wild ride so far, but have *you* considered the legacy you will leave behind?

UNFORGETTABLE HEROES!

Now faith is the substance of things hoped for, the evidence of things not seen. By faith we understand that the worlds were framed by the word of God, so that the things which are seen were not made of things which are visible (Heb. 11:1, 3 NKJV).

The first chapter of Hebrews gives testimony to the lives of so many biblical heroes of the faith. By faith, Abel's worthy of-

Running Into "Happily Ever After"

fering was accepted by God as a better sacrifice than Cain's. By faith, Enoch pleased God so much that he was taken to heaven without ever experiencing death. By faith, Noah preserved the circle of life for future generations through his obedience in building an unexplainable ark for his own family and that preposterous zoo. By faith, Abraham left his homeland to live as a stranger in a foreign country. By faith, Sarah gave birth to a son in her old age and Abraham literally became the father of many nations. By faith, Abraham passed God's test as he lay his precious son Isaac on an altar of sacrifice. By faith, Isaac blessed Jacob and Esau. By faith, Jacob bestowed God's blessing on each of Joseph's sons. By faith, Joseph foretold of the Israelites' exodus from Egypt. By faith, Moses' parents defied the king's decree to kill all baby boys. By faith, Moses gave up his privilege and inheritance in Pharoah's house and kingdom to lead his own people out of Egypt. By faith, the Israelites crossed the Red Sea on dry land and later marched around the city of Jericho until the walls came tumbling down without a sword drawn. By faith, Rahab the prostitute gave refuge to spies and was shown mercy. By faith, so many lived and died and are remembered even today.

Did you notice what each and every one of these pioneers had in common, the legacy that has lasted long after they have gone from this world? Though their bodies have rotted away long ago in ancient graves, they have passed their treasure of faith to generations that follow after them. What kind of faith is this that it would drive them with such determination? What kind of faith do you have?

Each one of these people of faith died not yet having in hand what was promised, but still believing. How did they do it? They saw it way off in the distance, waved their greeting, and accepted the fact that they were transients in this world. People who live this way make it plain that they are looking for their true home. If they were homesick for the old country, they could have gone back any time they wanted. But they were after a far better country than that—heaven country. You can see why God is so proud of them, and has a City waiting for them (Heb. 11:13-16 MSG).

I am convinced that everything that has a date of birth is also stamped with a date of expiration. One thing was certain way back then and is so even today—with the exception of Enoch of course—the ratio of births to deaths is one to one. As sure as we are born, we are also sure to die, so what do we hang onto? The substance of things hoped for and the evidence of things unseen. Those who went before us believed in God's promise, an eternal hope, and their legacy of faith has been handed down through the generations to us.

What does the word "legacy" mean to you? The *American Heritage Dictionary* defines the word as "something handed down from an ancestor or a predecessor or from the past." So what has been handed down to you from the past? Think about it—family heirlooms, wealth and possessions, notable position in society and politics (like the Kennedys or Bushes), ethnic culture and customs, family traditions, and even genetic traits and abilities like blue eyes and musical talent as well as strong bones or heart disease. And don't forget those intangibles such as values, beliefs, and Christian faith. And now, I ask myself and you an even greater question. What are we as Christian leaders and examples handing down to the generations that follow us?

What kind of legacies are we leaving behind, and how do they impact the future? We can leave those tangible physical things like money, possessions, and heirlooms; but in the end, those things really can't go beyond the earthly grave. Those are the things that "moth and rust" can corrupt. Jesus said, "But store up for yourselves treasures in heaven, where moth and rust do not destroy, and where thieves do not break in and steal. For where your treasure is, there your heart will be also" (Matt. 6:20-21 NIV). What really counts is the only legacy that lasts beyond the grave and beyond this world, drawing others who come behind us into eternity—our faith.

While I was a graduate student at Hardin Simmons University, one of the professors asked us to introduce ourselves on the first day of class by sharing our favorite life quote. Most of the students gave wise and honorable sentiments and proverbs, but the not-so-traditional student who sat next to me gave the most memorable. Dustin had never been accused of being the "teacher's pet," and he was still there only by grace. In fact, before this graduate semester, he had been advised not to return until he seriously considered the direction his life was taking. Ironically, he returned as a campus dorm director, and he unveiled the wisdom that a widow had spoken into his life, "Son, the only thing that lives on after you die is what you give to another man's soul." Years have passed but those words stuck to me like glue. I strive to live that widow's advice through my own favorite quote and life motto, "Live to love." What do you give to another man's soul?

Torchbearers of Hope

In my high school days, as I mentioned earlier, I served as a volunteer coach for the local Special Olympics tennis team and accompanied them to the state meet in Austin. My intentions then were not so noble as they may seem because I was actually seeking the affections of yet another pretty girl, a fellow volunteer coach. I think, though, that some of the values of the

Special Olympics may have stuck with me. One of the most honored symbols of the World Games is the Flame of Hope, which was carried by more than 85,000 law enforcement officers throughout the world in the Law Enforcement Torch Run across thirty-five countries in 2007 to raise awareness and funds for the World Games. The flame is symbolic of the mission and hope that the Special Olympics will give a voice and purpose to those with intellectual disabilities. In the games, these special athletes are inspired and empowered to rise above their difficulties to participate and compete in the Special Olympic games. Along the way, these challenged athletes not only improve in physical and motor skills, they also grow in self-confidence and joy, reaching their full potential as they grow mentally, socially, and spiritually. They are given hope and in turn, they give hope to others. Severely challenged—yes, but leaders in their own right!

On April 13, 1997 I surrendered my life to the ministry of the gospel of Jesus Christ. It was on that day that I first heard the story of the dying grandmother who prayed that Jesus would spare the life of her infant grandson and the rest of the prayer that followed, "And Jesus, will you put a calling on his life that he will never reject?" It was seventeen years later, but God finally answered her fateful prayer on that spring day in 1997. You see, that praying grandmother was my grandmother, and I was the grandson whose life was saved. Because of her strong faith and enduring hope, God wanted to do so much more than just spare my life. I never knew my grandmother, but she left me her legacy of faith through that prayer and I realized it the day I surrendered to His call. By faith, my grandmother carried her own flame of hope in Jesus Christ that others would share the hope that He had given her. And she passed that flame to me through her prayer as she completed the last leg of her own life

Running Into "Happily Ever After"

marathon. Today, I carry that same flame of hope as I live out the calling Christ has placed on my life. I am both humbled and honored to carry on my grandmother's legacy of faith, and I strive to carry her torch on to eternity with me, lighting the way for others who come behind me.

As I look back over my life, I am conscious of the truth that there are so many beautiful people who have given so much to my own soul—each one of them a torchbearer in their own right. Though my grandmother didn't live to teach me how to carry the flame, God sent another amazing woman of faith into my life and ministry to show me just how to run the race and carry the torch through her own example. Pat Nickel instilled in me a deep compassion for the outcasts of this world as both of us served as volunteers at a local homeless ministry for which I would eventually serve as a staff member for over eight years. As we combed the Abilene community to feed and meet the physical and spiritual needs of the homeless, Pat would literally jump out of the ministry van before I could brake just to catch the attention of a homeless man walking down the alley. Not only did she teach me to love people, but she also exemplified the love of Christ in the way she loved me. As I began to travel, speaking to audiences across the country, Pat would call my cell phone about an hour before I was scheduled to speak without fail. She would say, "Chad, I don't want to keep you long. I know you're getting ready to speak, but I want you to know that I love you and I am praying for you."

One Sunday Pat wasn't at church and her friend Donnice, another older woman of faith told me that Pat hadn't come to pick her up that morning, and she couldn't reach her. Just the day before, Pat had insisted on visiting those in the church neighborhood even though she didn't feel well. I instinctively knew something was wrong. I grabbed Eli, a law enforcement officer who attended our church, and we went to her home. We knocked on the door but received no answer. Through the window, I saw her lying on the floor with the phone receiver in her hand. Eli kicked in the locked door, but we were too late. She had died of heart failure. In that sobering moment, I was forced to face the loss of one of my greatest heroes of faith. Her family gave me a ton of plastic canvas small crosses that Sister Pat had made to give to people who gave their lives to the Lord. To this very day, I still hand out those crosses to people who are truly allowing God to transform their lives. Her journey was completed when she crossed the finish line in death, but the legacy of loving faith she carried so masterfully in life still remains in me and in all the other beautiful people she encountered on the streets of Abilene, Texas. I still miss her phone calls when I travel across the country to speaking engagements, but the love of Christ that Sister Pat shared so freely in life lives on and still grows within me and through me. Her flame of hope lives eternally through that love.

HOPE'S BLAZE LIVES ON!

My grandmother's prayerful legacy ignited my torch of faith, and Pat's loving legacy keeps that fire burning. Through what I have learned from my own personal heroes of faith and through those ancient heroes in the Bible, I understand the legacy of knowledge and faith that Paul left to Timothy in his letters. In 2 Timothy 2, he gave explicit guidelines to keep our flames of hope burning so we can pass them on to the next generation.

First, he reminded Timothy and us that our identity is found solely in Christ. "You then, my son, be strong in the grace that is in Christ Jesus" (2 Tim. 2:1 NIV). In Greek context, the word "strong" in this verse specifically means, "to be continually strengthened," not in our own knowledge or ability but in Christ alone. Several years back my father was diagnosed with kidney cancer. We can't avoid it these days; most of us are inescapably touched by cancer at some point in our lives—either personally or through a loved one or a dear friend. I just never thought it would be my dad! He has always been strong, healthy, and active and as his son, I suppose I wanted to think he was invincible—another Superman. The news shocked all of us—I was devastated. But I wasn't just his son; I was also his pastor. How do you combine the two roles? This disease was an intruder in our lives, and it hit too close to home this time. My dad is a man of very few words but we talked about cancer. I was seeking to comfort my dad, but his words to me gave me an inexpressible sweet joy as he assured me where he stood, "Son, I talk about having faith. Now it's time to prove it."

    I knew that, no matter what the outcome of cancer would be, my dad would be okay. In just a few words, my dad assured me that his identity was not found in cancer but in Christ alone. He had one of his kidneys removed, rarely letting any of us see his pain and discomfort. And in the months following as he waited and watched for the cancer to return, he lived out Paul's encouragement to Timothy. I've watched him stand stronger in his faith than I have ever seen before, and I think I also grew stronger. It was almost as if my dad were encouraging me as Paul did Timothy, "Son, be strong in the faith that is in Christ Jesus." He has survived cancer thus far, but every six months he has to have a check up to make sure that dreaded enemy hasn't returned. I would never wish cancer on anyone, and I don't believe God brings it on us. But I do know that in my dad, and in other close friends who have faced cancer and survived, God has used even this enemy for His glory as their strength in grace becomes evident to all. My dad isn't invincible, but he is eternally saved by his faith. When he goes in for tests and scans every six months and once again we face our worst fear that the cancer will be back, I am reminded that my dad's faith isn't just talk. He lives his life in Christ alone.

Paul's second key to building a legacy and keeping hope alive is to share the hope we have received with others so they too can light the way for even more. "And the things you have heard me say in the presence of many witnesses entrust to reliable men who will also be qualified to teach others" (2 Tim. 2:2 NIV). The key word "entrust" should jump out at you; it means to trust someone else with something valuable. We don't run this marathon alone—not even in ministry. Paul urges us to carry the flame of hope even farther with the help of reliable men. From time to time, I laugh at business gimmicks based on pyramid schemes because so often they don't work. But have you ever considered where the original pyramid sales theory came from? It comes straight from Scripture. Jesus held the hope of salvation, and He shared it with twelve reliable men, His disciples. And they in turn followed His great commission to go into all the world and teach others what He had taught them. Jesus is the Flame of Hope, and He gave twelve men a torch which they carried far and wide lighting more torches that still burn today.

Lauren McCain, one of the slain victims in the Virginia Tech massacre on April 16, 2007, still carried her Flame of Hope. Her myspace page inspired thousands for a long while after her death. She said of herself in her bio, "The purpose and love of my life is Jesus Christ. I don't have to argue religion, philosophy, or historical evidence because I *know* Him." (Lauren McCain's myspace profile ID has since been deleted.) She didn't just know about Him, she knew Him personally and she knows Him now in eternity. Proving that Lauren's Flame of Hope was still burning in the lives of others, her friend Casey commented on Lauren's page after her death, "You inspired so many because you lived like a real Christian. Your impact on so many lives, including my own, is astounding. You really loved God and now you can finally dance before Him. I love you, Lauren." Her torch still burns because she didn't just talk about her faith, she lived it even in death.

"Endure hardship with us like a good soldier of Christ Jesus" (2 Tim. 2:3 NIV). Another difficult truth in keeping hope's flame alive is that we must recognize that our journey as a torchbearer cannot be accomplished without sacrifice. We see the many sacrifices of those heroes of faith who have gone before us:

> *By faith these people overthrew kingdoms, ruled with justice, and received what God had promised them. They shut the mouths of lions, quenched the flames of fire, and escaped death by the edge of the sword. Their weakness was turned to strength. They became strong in battle and put whole armies to flight. Women received their loved ones back again from death. But others were tortured, refusing to turn from God in order to be set free. They placed their hope in a better life after the resurrection. Some were jeered at, and their backs were cut open with whips. Others were chained in prisons. Some died by stoning, some were sawed in half, and others were killed with the sword. Some went about wearing skins of sheep and goats, destitute and oppressed and mistreated. They were too good for this world, wandering over deserts and mountains, hiding in caves and holes in the ground. All these people earned a good reputation because of their faith, yet none of them received all that God had promised. For God had something better in mind for us, so that they would not reach perfection without us* (Heb. 11:33-40 NLT).

No, God never promised us a rose garden. Even Paul, one of the greatest heroes of the faith, spoke far more about thorns than he ever did about roses! But the hope we have in God's perpetually unfolding plan is worth the sacrifices we make along the way.

"No one serving as a soldier gets involved in civilian affairs—he wants to please his commanding officer. Similarly, if anyone competes as an athlete, he does not receive the victor's crown unless he competes according to the rules" (2 Tim. 2:4-5 NIV). Especially as pastors and Christian leaders, we must follow where Christ leads—in the trail He has so purposely blazed before us. And we cannot stray from His path to go chasing rabbits or butterflies along the way because we can only receive the victorious prize if we follow the rules He has set before us and finish the race. We must keep our focus only on Him and let go of the torch of faith only when we have reached the end of our journey.

"The hardworking farmer should be the first to receive a share of the crops. Remember Jesus Christ, raised from the dead, descended from David" (2 Tim. 2:6, 8 NIV). Paul cautions us with his firm advice to run the marathon with diligent perseverance, holding our torch high so that we may receive the first share of the reward God has promised. Those runners who become distracted or who dillydally, wasting time and energy, risk the life of the flame of hope. It flickers and dims in their carelessness as their oil that fuels the flame burns away. But those who run faithfully at a steady pace uphill, downhill, and around every twist and turn, keep their torch raised heavenward, always pointing to Jesus Christ. He alone is the center of our lives as His legacy lives in us. He is the everlasting fuel that keeps the flame of hope alive as it burns into eternity. We seek Him first in everything because He is truly the Lord of our lives.

Jesus offered a beautiful testimony of such a flamebearer at the home of Simon the Leper in Bethany. As the men reclined around the table, a woman entered carrying a beautiful alabaster box filled with expensive perfume. She approached Jesus and broke the jar. Then by faith, in an act of true worship, she poured the pure nard over His head. Others in the room were indignant and rebuked her flagrant waste. That jar of costly oil was worth a year's wages and could have fed the poor and hungry for months! But Jesus knew her heart and she knew His. The men in the room had heard virtually every word He had spoken yet they still didn't understand. This woman of worship recognized the genuine gift of His presence and the impending loss. As she poured her precious oil over Him, she also raised her flame of hope to the Lamb, to the Lord and King of her heart. Jesus chastised the men, "Leave her alone. Why criticize her for doing such a good thing to me? You will always have the poor among you, and you can help them whenever you want to. But you will not always have me. She has done what she could and has anointed my body for burial ahead of time. I tell you the truth, wherever the Good News is preached throughout the world, this woman's deed will be remembered and discussed" (Mark 14:3-9 NLT).

What an amazing legacy she has left in worship! Though her act was hardly noble by worldly standards, she pointed to Him. She remembered Christ, only Christ. The men fussed over the waste, despairing over the meals the money would have bought, but she clung to the eternal hope she found in her Savior. Their flames of hope flickered and dimmed, but hers shone bright and strong, lighting the way for those who come behind her.

And finally Paul offers us his last and most crucial word of advice in carrying the torch of faith while keeping the flame of hope, the legacy, alive through his own testimony, "Therefore I endure everything for the sake of the elect, that they too may obtain the salvation that is in Christ Jesus, with eternal glory" (2 Tim. 2:10 NIV). Once again, he uses the term "endure," urging us to run the race to the very finish no matter what. Never give up! It would be so easy to give up in our calling and in our ministry. We don't always get to see the fruits of our labor, but we are promised that our labor is not in vain. Once again, we are reminded as Christian leaders that it's not about us. We finish for the sake of those who come behind us so that we may pass the legacy of hope on to future generations. It doesn't matter who comes in first, or third, or dead last. Paul never said we must finish first although Jesus had plenty to say about first place, "The first shall be last and the last shall be first" (Luke 13:30 NIV).

What is most important is that we keep playing the game of life until the very last second ticks past and the final buzzer sounds. In the Special Olympics, every athlete who overcomes his personal challenges, who gives his all until the very last second and completes his event, is a winner. At the finish line there are no losers, only winners. In the same way, a crown of victory awaits any of us who endures the journey of faith, overcoming every obstacle, and keeping the flame of hope held high toward heaven and burning brightly until we run through the ribbon at the finish line. Our legacy of hope lives and is ready to be passed to the next runner for his leg of the journey of faith. As the laurel wreath is placed on our heads, we pass the flame to those who come behind us. How beautiful are the feet of those who are dedicated to share the Good News of Christ and who persevere in that race.

Therefore, since we are surrounded by such a great cloud of witnesses, let us throw off everything that hinders and the sin that so easily entangles, and let us run with perseverance the race marked out for us. Let us fix our eyes on Jesus, the author and perfecter of our faith (Heb. 12:1-2 NIV).

LEGACIES LIVING AMONG US

As I look around my church congregation, I see amazing testimonies of lives lived in faith as the legacy of hope shines in our Mission family. My grandmother's legacy lives on in me, but I've also had the honor and privilege of seeing the legacy of hope from those who went before us passed on to the new generations. Hope lives on in them.

The Mission is blessed with an awesome worship team, and their gift of worship with us shines just as brightly as the music of the most renowned band who has sold countless records. Christ lives and shines through each team member. I had the honor of seeing that beautiful legacy handed down to our worship leader, Steve, at the celebration of his mother's life well-lived in faith. Catherine was a longtime faithful member of Pioneer Drive Baptist Church, which gave birth to our own church, Mission Abilene, passing the flame of hope on to a brand new Body in Christ. For many years, Catherine was the loved and cherished church organist at her home church where Steve grew up. Catherine was a classic church musician. She dedicated her life to the gift of worship she shared with her church and with her children.

So few of us truly understand the significance of the dedication and passion of the church musicians because their presence is always constant. On Sunday mornings, we don't see the many sacrifices they make in rehearsals and prayerful planning for worship. Year after year, Catherine attended rehearsals, meetings, and events for the sake of worship. She never refused when asked to serve in faithfulness to the calling God had placed on her life. As a young boy, Steve played in the hallways and the sidewalks of Pioneer Drive Baptist Church while his mother lived out her legacy. Without even realizing it, the flame began to grow in him. Most of us at the Mission never even saw the torch his mother carried as she ran her journey ahead of him. The gift they have shared is a valuable and rare treasure just like the precious perfume the woman poured over Jesus' head in Bethany.

Recognizing the legacy that Pioneer Drive Baptist Church gave in birth of the Mission, I also saw a beautiful flame of hope passed from one generation to another at Catherine's memorial celebration after she had crossed the finish line in her own journey of faith. Every ounce of passion and love in music that she shared with her own family and her church now lives in Steve. He shares it with us each Sunday morning as he sings and plays his acoustic guitar with the Mission Band. Her faith and legacy of hope lives on in the beauty of Steve's worship and praise. His own life and music is a living tribute to the faithful one who went ahead of him.

There's also an amazing group of young men who continually hold their flames of hope high as they lift them in praise to Christ every Sunday in response to Steve and the rest of the Mission Band's gift of worship. Oh, their voices aren't nearly so finely tuned or skilled. They may sing off-key and their harmony may not blend so harmoniously with the melody of praise sung by our worship team. One of them passionately plays his air guitar each week, and another occasionally plays his air drums. Oh, these boys may not sing the right words or even real words at all as we perceive them, but their sounds of joy and praise are every bit as beautiful and treasured as the Mission

Band's most perfect song. You see, these boys are severely challenged both mentally and physically. They reside in one of the group homes for the severely disabled. They began attending our worship services within the past year but have quickly become very precious members of our family of faith. In tenderness and utmost patience, the dedicated attendants who accompany them to church each Sunday share their own personal faith and legacies of hope with these honored children of God each and every day. The flame of hope that burns so brightly in them shines all around our congregation as the boys' rowdy and unrefined amens and hallelujah praises echo in our services each week. And not one of us on the ministry team, the Mission Band, or among the congregation would have it any other way! In their abounding joy, these boys show us the true significance of worship in the presence of the Lord and King of our hearts. I believe Jesus honors and treasures their worship with joy because of their oblivion to the people who surround them. They raise their torches to Christ, the Lamb of Glory, in genuine worship and faith. The challenges and obstacles each boy faces are great and may often seem insurmountable, but each one runs his own race at his own pace with courage and perseverance, and each one of these unique heroes of faith will reach his own finish line as a cloud of witnesses cheers him on to victory.

WE WERE HERE!

Those ancient heroes of the faith are still remembered even ages beyond the lives they lived on this earth. So many beautiful and distinct legacies live on in the hearts of our Mission family. And by faith, just as those who have gone before did, each one in our congregation is making a way for those who will come behind them. As each legacy lives and grows, we know that one day our eternal hope will be passed as our legacy to those who come behind us. Just as my grandmother's and Pat Nickel's presence remains in me and Catherine's presence lives on in Steve, I know that each one of our Mission living legacies are leaving their own mark on the world of tomorrow.

I consider those lives which have made their mark on my own. Looking back through the years, I can see all those people who so willingly sacrificed as they wove their legacies into the tapestry of my life, each one leaving his/her own heirloom thread of hope in me in some manner or another. Their legacies remained behind so that I would pick up their torch of faith and carry hope's flame for those who come after me. Each one of them made me who I am today. My grandmother's faithfulness in prayer, Pat Nickel's passion for the down and out, Lauren McCain's knowledge of the intimate friend she found in Christ, even Dustin's revelation of the gifts we give to men's souls, and so many more. Each one of them impacted my faith and my life has been forever changed.

And suddenly, I wonder about the impact I have on the lives of others. How brightly does my torch of faith shine around me? Have I woven threads of hope into the life tapestries of others? One day when I have crossed the finish line into eternity, will there be a ripple that remains? Will future generations remember that I was here as they remember the lives of Noah and Abraham and Moses?

MY HOPE OF GLORY

I've spent my entire life hearing that He has set eternity in the hearts of men, and I always thought that eternity was the hope of an everlasting life in heaven. So often, that eternity has been explained as though we live and exist in this life in hope of the reward we receive at the end of our journey. But honestly, I just don't find myself sitting around and wondering what it's going to be like walking around on streets of gold and living in a glorious mansion in a heavenly city beyond the sunset. Not that it's wrong for you, but it just never seemed quite right for me. I don't dwell in that heavenbound mentality, in that longing for home—I have to live in the present. But as I consider the thought of reaching the finish line of my own personal journey of faith, I don't just think about the end of the race. As I cross that line and that laurel wreath is finally placed on my head, I look to those who come behind me and finally I lower my torch—that flame of hope which I have faithfully held high toward Christ, who sits at God's right hand. And I hand my torch to the generation who is just beginning their leg of this marathon. I give to them the same legacy of hope that was passed down to me. As I prepare to pass my own torch, I have to recognize what I really hope for.

In truth, God has given me an eternal hope, and He has promised that at the end of my journey I too will receive my own crown of glory and an everlasting inheritance in heaven. His promise has been guaranteed and sealed. But that reward is not the eternal hope for which I have lived. Suddenly, Paul's words to Timothy have a new significance in the light of eternity. What was his final admonition to Timothy as he carried his torch of faith across the finish line? Read it once more: "Therefore I endure everything for the sake of the elect that they too may obtain the salvation that is in Christ Jesus, with eternal glory." Paul persevered through so many trials and struggles, but he didn't run that race for the purpose of his own gain. That was not his eternal hope. Paul lived each day with the purpose of sharing the Christ within, his own Hope of Glory, with others so that they too may receive salvation from the very same Christ. Paul's eternal hope was not in heaven's reward but in Christ alone.

The Superman Syndrome

So many of us compare the seen and unseen things Paul spoke of so passionately, and we get it all wrong sometimes. Paul lays it out before us, but we don't get it until we consider what he meant when he endured "for the sake of the elect." Those things we see, touch, and feel in this life are only temporary and have no impact beyond their existence on earth. Health, beauty, finances, possessions, achievements—none of that gets beyond the grave. Those unseen things are the intangible things of the Holy Spirit that last far beyond death. How we live for Christ, how we love, and how we draw others to Him are what really matter, and they impact eternity as they transform the hearts of those with whom we share own great hope.

There are many songs and much preaching about one day walking on golden streets. I don't believe that is what God or Paul intended. My eternal reward does not affect how I live today. It's just an unfathomable dream until it happens. I have no doubt that I will be filled with joy unspeakable when that dream finally comes true.

In setting our minds on things above rather than things below, I believe Paul is telling us to focus on those intangible words, acts, and sacrifices we make along our journey that will impact eternity and not on the cares of this world that don't even matter. What we do or how we love and live when the Holy Spirit dwells in us—those acts and sacrifices will impact eternity as they instill the message of grace and salvation in the hearts of those who come after us. We should focus much less on those things we can't take with us that won't really make a difference in eternity anyway. The car I drive, the balance in my checkbook, and the title on my deskplate don't change a thing for eternity. But those intangible words and acts which point others to my own Hope of Glory—those matter. Loving like Jesus loved, true worship of the One who created us, genuine repentance, renewing the mind, and sharing Christ's message of grace with my own child and the lost within my circle of reach—those things make a difference for eternity because they point to Christ.

In those special moments, I know that I have shared the legacy of hope with others and lit their flame of hope as they run beside me or behind me in this race of life. By setting our minds on things above, we discover His higher ways and higher thoughts, and we relish in them and then share them with those who follow. We are lighting the flame of hope for others and planting eternity into the hearts of men.

I finally realize that my discomfort in fantasizing about my days in heaven is not wrong or even weird. As Jesus patterned for us in His own life, I realize that we aren't supposed to waste our time dreaming of forever yet to come. Time and again, Jesus encouraged us to focus on today, not tomorrow, because what we do today in this very moment can impact another's eternity. For those who come behind us, their eternal reward may not yet be guaranteed or sealed because the Hope of Glory, Jesus Christ, does not yet dwell in their hearts.

That makes much more sense to me than pining for life after death. My everlasting life is already promised to me, and that's what I can hold onto when others tell me that I should set my mind on things above. And Christ within me, my everlasting Hope of Glory is what I strive to leave with those who come behind me.

Passing the Flame

A few months ago, Sheri and I shared an email conversation about being eternity minded—about heaven. Though she holds to the faith that Christ is her Hope of Glory, she was struggling with her own beliefs about heaven, and she asked me if I ever actually pictured or imagined myself in heaven. At the Mission, our hearts rejoice and tears sting our eyes when we sing the words to "I Can Only Imagine," especially as we think of those precious ones in our church family who have already crossed their finish line and received their victorious crowns. I told her that I believed at the moment of death, we enter into God's presence, but honestly I couldn't say that I could actually fathom the reality of that moment. Still not comprehending the concept of eternity mindedness, she asked if I was confident that eternity was something to hope for.

This past year, I preached a sermon series about eternity: "If I Die Before I Wake" hoping to dispel doubts and misunderstandings about eternity. The truths laid out were difficult to preach—hell and heaven—and even more difficult for the congregation to hear. I was already planning this sermon series when I became aware of her own struggle in faith and in her lifelong battle with the conflicting messages and beliefs regarding eternity. I committed to pray for her. On the Sunday that I preached about our last moment in death and our first moment in eternity, the Holy Spirit began to speak to her heart even in the beginning of the morning's worship before I stepped on the stage to speak.

As the service began and the Mission Band sang, "When I Survey the Wondrous Cross," all the scattered pieces of her faith and brokenness came into view. That wondrous Cross, the passion and purpose of Christ, repentance, worship, and yes, even eternity, all fell into place and bound rightly together like a beautiful mosaic. As I began to speak that morning, I explained what I believe happens in the very moment of death. She tried to tune me out, rebellious of a message about eternity and fearful of what it meant for her. In her own quest to understand, she had already studied the Scriptures that I was sharing in the days and weeks before, completely unaware of the message I would share this particular Sunday. No doubt the Spirit had guided her search. She didn't want to hear it, but as I quoted the same Scriptures she had studied, the familiar words echoed in her head. And the more I shared, the clearer her own mosaic portrait of grace became.

I shared that in the final moment of death—our first moment in eternity—we simply enter into the Lord's holy presence. Finally, the light began to dawn, and Sheri found the truth she needed to hold onto. Pearly gates, streets of gold, mansions—all that is just fluff to her and the necessity of believing or hoping for eternity just didn't make sense. But His presence—His sweet presence—that really matters. Finally, she began to think about crossing her own finish line in the moment of death. A little eternal mindedness crept in unaware and the reality of an everlasting hope finally sunk in her heart. No matter what had been drilled into Sheri's head her entire life, she finally realized and accepted that her eternal hope did not lie in all of heaven's "fluff," the eternal rewards. Her true Hope for eternity resides where it always has—Christ within her, the Hope of Glory. In the dawn of that revelation for her, I realize that her own flame of hope finally caught fire. Christ's presence was suddenly very real, and the blaze of her own hope began to burn strongly, steadily, and brightly. From my own torch of faith to hers, I realize in my message of hope, I've been blessed to share and pass along the everlasting Flame of Hope as both of us continue on our individual and intertwined journeys of faith.

FIND US FAITHFUL

In our human brokenness, each one of us—and yes, even those who live by faith—sometimes look for reasons to keep on in this life. So often, we can't see beyond our circumstances, our fears, and our failures, and we are overwhelmed. As leaders, we often reflect on those we lost who turned away from faith along the way, and we focus on our failures rather than our victories. Even the prospect of attempting to leave a legacy that can impact forever seems impossible. But remember, our hope is not in what we do or even say. Our eternal hope is simply Jesus Christ, the Lord and King of our hearts. Our legacies are not built by our own accomplishments. The legacies we leave behind us can only be built by Jesus Christ within us. Leaving a legacy of hope—sharing Christ our eternal hope—should be the purpose of any ministry, of any single life that has truly been given and surrendered to Him. In essence, sharing hope's flame is what Christ has created each and every one of us to do.

As a cloud of heroic and faithful witnesses cheer us on, by faith we are to use those many threads that have been woven into our lives by those who went before us. We can be a living legacy for our children and an eternal legacy for our children's children and their children. Just as someone has sown their hope into us, we continually sow into others, reaching souls that will share in the same eternity because we were willing to share His message. Christ has called each one of us to use all that God has given us to "set eternity in the hearts of men." I pray that we will be remembered ages hence because our lives were well-lived in faith. We must remember, however, that our legacy isn't just the memory we leave behind. Our true legacy is the Hope that we instill in the hearts of those who come behind us. Our legacy is not found in our ability to don our Superman capes so that we may achieve or overcome the impossible. Our only goal is to lift up our Savior above all else so that we may point others to Him. Our living and lasting legacy *is* Jesus Christ and only Christ. May all those who come behind us find us faithful because He is forever faithful.

Running Into "Happily Ever After"

STUDY QUESTIONS

1. What does the word "legacy" mean to you?
_____
_____
_____

2. What legacies have been handed down to you from people in your past?
_____
_____
_____

3. What are you presently giving to other people's souls?
_____
_____
_____

4. How do you live a life of sacrifice as you journey through life as a torchbearer?
_____
_____
_____

5. What legacy will you leave behind?
_____
_____
_____

About the Author

Chad Mitchell has a B.B.S. in psychology and a M.Ed. in Counseling and Human Development from Hardin Simmons University of Abilene, Texas. Chad is a licensed and ordained Minister of the Gospel, but above all, his greatest and most necessary qualification is that God called him!

Chad is a gifted communicator who passionately speaks from the Word of God. He currently serves as lead pastor of Mission Abilene, a church that focuses on loving the underdogs and outcasts of society. He passionately pursues those who are forgotten or deemed unreachable, showing them that the love of God reaches all. He is unswerving in his devotion to stand against injustice and to empower the homeless, the addicted, the battered and beaten, and the convicted to rise above their circumstances through salvation and discipleship.

In the spring of 1997, Chad surrendered his life to full-time ministry, and since then his unique, straightforward speaking style has given him the privilege to speak in hundreds of different settings all over Texas and much of the U.S. at youth camps and rallies, Disciple Now events, Christian concerts, crusades, citywide revivals, church services, and street outreaches.

He is passionate about spreading the truth and grace of God's story far and wide to all who need a message of hope and redemption, not just through the spoken word but also the written word. This year, he has broadened the horizons of his ministry through writing. His second book, *Beyond Plastic Christianity*, will be published in the fall of 2009.

Chad Mitchell and his wife, Ashley, have one daughter, Alexis. His family lives and serves in ministry in Abilene, Texas.

Contact Information

To contact Chad Mitchell, please visit his website at www.chadmitchell.org